THE ROCKY MOUNTAINS

Lazy K Bar Ranch, Big Timber, Montana

COUNTRY INNS OF AMERICA

The Rocky Mountains

A GUIDE TO THE INNS OF
COLORADO, UTAH, NEVADA, IDAHO, WYOMING, AND MONTANA

BY TERRY BERGER

PHOTOGRAPHED BY FRED AND DOROTHY BUSK

WITH ADDITIONAL PHOTOGRAPHS BY GEORGE W. GARDNER AND PHILIP LIEF

DESIGNED BY ROBERT REID

HOLT, RINEHART AND WINSTON, *New York*

AN OWL BOOK

Front cover: The Greyhouse Inn, Salmon,
Idaho.

Frontispiece: Imperial Hotel, Cripple Creek,
Colorado. The piano in the Thirst Parlour bar on which
Max Morath played his famous ragtime music
from 1950 to 1959.

Back cover: Monument Valley, Utah.

Map by Anthony St. Aubyn.

Copyright © 1983 by Holt, Rinehart and Winston
All rights reserved, including the right to reproduce this
book or portions thereof in any form.
Published by Holt, Rinehart and Winston, 383 Madison
Avenue, New York, New York 10017.
Published simultaneously in Canada by
Holt, Rinehart and Winston of Canada, Limited.

Library of Congress Cataloging in Publication Data

Berger, Terry.
  The Rocky Mountains.

  (Country inns of America)
  "An Owl book."
  1. Hotels, taverns, etc.—Rocky Mountains Region—
Directories. I. Busk, Fred T.   II. Busk, Dorothy.
III. Title   IV. Series.
TX907.B43 1983   647'.97801   82-21167
ISBN 0-03-062211-5

First Edition

10 9 8 7 6 5 4 3 2 1

A Robert Reid—Wieser & Wieser Production

Printed in the United States of America

ISBN 0-03-062211-5

THE INNS

EDITOR'S NOTE

There are 45 inns described and illustrated in this book. Our photographer and writer visited them all and selected them as outstanding for various reasons: historical interest, food, ambience, innkeepers, furnishings, local amenities. Each inn offers a different mix of characteristics, so study them carefully to determine which ones you might most enjoy. All inngoers have strong personal preferences, and there are inns represented here to suit all tastes.

The five lodges in Montana's Glacier National Park are covered. For people interested in seeing this grand country, they are useful to know about, and are themselves hold-overs from an earlier day when monumental log and stone construction was *de rigeur*.

Visting a country inn for the first time requires a certain spirit of adventure. Usually an inn is far nicer than we can describe it, but it is also possible for changes to occur since we were there—chefs come and go, staff changes occur—but generally these are temporary, and a visit is usually worthwhile at any time. If not, let us know. And if we have omitted some personal favorites, again let us know so that we can look at them for future editions.

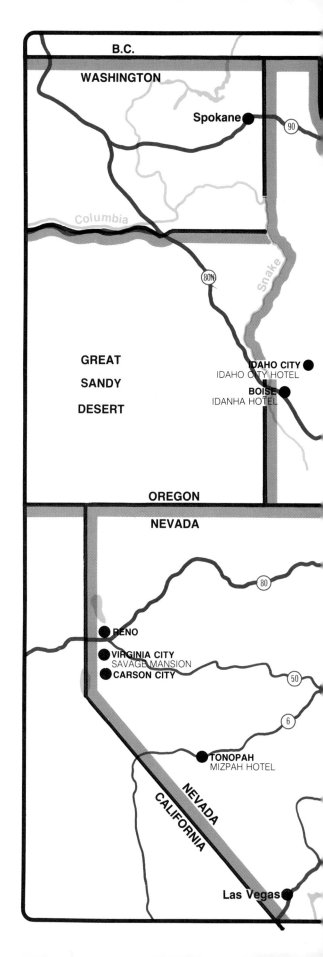

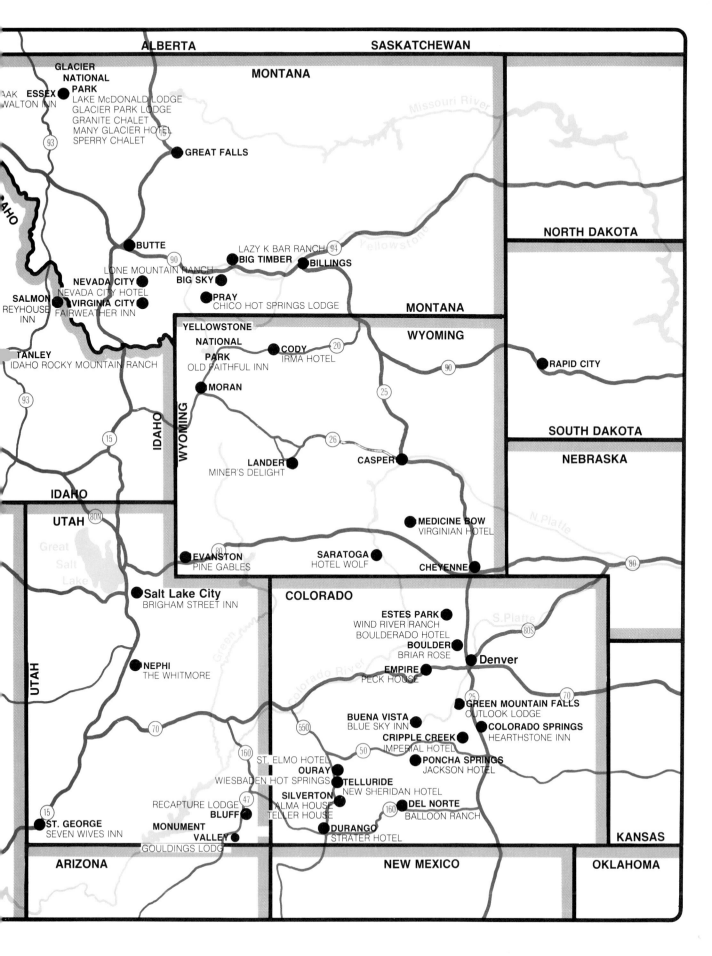

WIND RIVER RANCH

Estes Park   **COLORADO**

Make friends with people and horses

Located in Colorado's high country in beautiful Tahosa Valley, this guest ranch is 9200 feet above sea level, surrounded by towering snow-capped mountains. Whether you ride, hike, or swim, there is no escaping the majestic beauty.

The site, homesteaded in 1876, became a private ranch for the Merrills of Bobbs-Merrill publishers in the twenties. The wonderful ranch house they built with chinked logs and box car interior has an enormous stone fireplace, and additional weathered pine lodges, with period furniture and antique pieces, make Wind River Ranch both comfortable and distinctive.

No one blows a whistle here to direct social activities, but if you need a program there is plenty to do. In addition to horseback riding, there are cookouts, volley ball, shuffleboard, and square dancing. A once-a-week Western, bingo, and visits from a naturalist round out the activities. The Irvins, former guests themselves, have owned and managed the ranch for the past nine years. Presently, they are in the process of making a lake and plan to stock it with trout.

Except for cookouts, the three meals a day are served in the dining room to guests seated on ladder back chairs at a variety of antique tables. Stained glass insets in one wall let colorful patterns into the room, and Navajo rugs on the walls add warmth. There is an old Steinway piano standing at the ready,

The Navajo rug is one of many Indian artifacts displayed.

and Russia's foremost meteorologist played Tchaikowsky on it when he stayed here.

All riding is instructional in western equitation, and the various trails are suited to degrees of skill, with rides to Wind River Gulch, Long's Peak, and Wild Basin. Bruce Gilette, head wrangler, is a former working cowboy who helps those unfamiliar with horses to become at ease with them. He points out that every horse, like every person, has its own personality and disposition, and recommends moving slowly and talking gently, gradually getting to know a horse and its ways.

The Irvin family is firmly in the saddle at Wind River Ranch—they oversee everything and provide comfort for all. Their happy hour allows guests to relax and make friendships that often last a lifetime. Everything here is simple and unassuming, with good cause. There is no competing with the great Rocky Mountains.

A lady wrangler, one of the students who come from all over the country to work at the ranch each summer.

Left: Long's Peak towers 14,255 feet over the ranch house.

WIND RIVER RANCH, P.O. Box 3410, Estes Park, CO 80517; (303) 586-4212; The Irvin Family, Innkeepers. Guest ranch in Colorado's high country furnished with antique and Indian artifacts. Open June to mid-October. Thirty rooms divided between 11 cabins and ranch house, all with baths and individual thermostats. Rates: $425 to $450 single, $630 to 680 double, weekly. Daily rates available. All rates include 3 meals daily. Riding is extra. There is no bar serving liquor, guests may bring their own. Children under 12 yrs. $6 off. (Child care available ages 6–12.) No pets. Visa and MasterCard accepted. Horseback riding, swimming pool, ping pong, shuffleboard, volleyball, trout fishing, hiking, raft trips on river. Nearby there is golf, tennis, and skiing.

DIRECTIONS: From Boulder drive north on US 36 through Lyons to Estes Park. Take left onto Rte. 7, go south 8 miles. Ranch is on left side. Total distance from Boulder is about 45 miles.

Boulder deserves this wonderful hotel

The Boulderado, a hotel built and financed by the people of Boulder, is once again becoming a peoples' hotel under new owners Frank Day and Arthur Wong. Built at the turn of the century, it was the grand hotel that Boulder needed for its burgeoning commerce and tourism.

After years of changing fortunes, the hotel is once again becoming the place that tourists as well as the citizens of Boulder are seeking out: for a fund raising dinner and dance for the Boulder Philharmonic, as a headquarters for the Coors Bicycle Classic, for Nancy Spanier's Dance Company, which performed in its lobby.

The lobby is set up for people. There are clusters of charming Victorian chairs, loveseats, and marble-topped tables, arranged for easy conversation. Drinks can be ordered, as well as fare from the lobby's Oyster Bar. A stained-glass dome over the mezzanine covers most of the lobby's ceiling and adds warmth to the cherrywood staircases and paneling. There is always music in the background.

The mezzanine has its own bar, and chairs and tables arranged along the railings overlook the lobby. From four-thirty until two in the morning, there is a piano bar, and appetizers and desserts can be ordered up from Winston's, the newly refurbished restaurant.

Three meals a day are available at Winston's, the seafood grill and bar. White columned, with a center dais, it has banquettes and the original ceramic tile floor which is also underfoot in the lobby. Stained glass fanlight windows and turn-of-the-century sideboards and mirrors add warmth and charm. A variety of oyster, shrimp, crab, and scallop dishes are featured, as well as salads, poultry, and beef. It operates a separate dining room for smokers.

The Bar, off the lobby, was opened in 1969, after Boulder stopped being dry. Before that only beer with a 3.2% alcohol content was served, and there were no bars in this largely student-populated city. Students and singles now frequent Newcomb's Tavern in the hotel's basement to eat, drink, and watch entertainment in seven underground rooms.

Left: Original cherrywood and mahogany woodwork glistens under the colorful stained-glass dome that dominates the lobby.

Built in 1906 for $71,000.

Bedrooms are either one room or two-room suites, furnished in newly refinished period pieces. Suites have refrigerators, wet bars, and a sleeping sofa in the sitting room.

Future plans for the hotel include a Pasta Bar, Lobster Porch, and Sweet Shoppe—specialties that this young town wants. A hotel for the people is what the Boulderado is all about.

HOTEL BOULDERADO, 2115 13th St., Boulder, CO 80302; (303) 442-4344; Mary Ann Mahoney and Sid Anderson, Managers. Oldest hotel in downtown Boulder, recently luxuriously renovated into 42 rooms and suites. Open year round. Rates range from $45 to $85 single, $60 to $100 double for rooms and suites, all with private baths. Two restaurants serving all meals, shrimp and oyster bar, and 3 bars. Children under 12 free. No pets. Visa, MasterCard, American Express accepted. Live entertainment and video available in house. Nearby there are swimming pools, tennis courts, racquetball, golfing, seasonal festivals, theater, and shops, food, and fun in downtown Boulder Mall.

DIRECTIONS: From Denver on US 36 to Arapahoe Ave. and turn left. Follow to 13th St. Make left and go 4 blocks to Spruce and 13th St.

An inn that makes you feel special

Raised in plantation country near Richmond, Virginia, Emily Hunter, innkeeper and part owner, has brought the southern tradition of gracious hospitality to the Flatirons of the Rocky Mountains. Touches of Williamsburg green and ashes of rose appear outside the Victorian house and are echoed again and again in the rooms.

A profusion of flowers—lilacs, wisteria, peonies, pink poppies, and of course the briar rose—may be in the house or blooming in carefully tended gardens at the time of your visit.

Stopping at the inn is precisely that, a visit. It is like staying with your rich aunt when you are her favorite niece or nephew, being installed in her best guest room and having her pamper you. Before you arrive she will have placed fresh cut flowers and a bowl of fruit in your room, and she will have left a bit of chocolate on your pillow to sweeten your dreams. She will gladly bring you breakfast in bed or to the lace-covered dining room table, or she will feed you on the sun porch where grape vines brush against the windows. There is always fresh orange juice, French-style yogurt, hot croissants, and market blend coffee. At the Briar Rose you always feel loved and wanted.

As soon as you enter the foyer of this Victorian house you sense that it is special. The walnut lady's desk, French rose-velvet chair and matching footstool

are, in a word, elegant. So are the other furnishings throughout the inn, which are not always costly but *always* selected with exquisite taste, especially the fabrics and colors.

Each bedroom is a delight, with headboards draped in calico or sheeting, matching coverlets, and pillow shams atop queen size beds. Some of the rooms have built-ins, and furnishings may include antique French desks, oak washstands, gilt mirrors, side chairs, brass towel stands, or carved tables.

The guests at the inn are special too and provide a chance to broaden horizons. A businessman from Australia, a woman studying meditation, a fifties beat poet, or a man researching narrow gauge railroads are not unusual. Emily, who is deeply interested in the literature of the fifties, plans to hold poetry readings. She also plans to add a conservatory onto the house to add drama and scope to the "High Tea—High Brow" on Sunday afternoons that has become so popular here. In addition to guest musicians, the event features scones, pastries, raspberry jam, lemon curd, Devon double cream, and assorted tea sandwiches, all served to inn guests, friends, and residents of Boulder.

The Briar Rose was originally conceived of as the "guest room" for Boulder residents who had none. It is a blessing to be invited to Boulder by someone who can't put you up.

Left: Sunday's "High Tea — High Brow," classic in every sense, is fast becoming the social event of Boulder. OVERLEAF: Popular Red Rocks Amphitheater, outside of Denver, is a spectacular setting for stage attractions.

BRIAR ROSE BED AND BREAKFAST, 2151 Arapahoe Ave., Boulder, CO 80302; (303) 442-3007; Emily Hunter, Innkeeper; Carol Siems, Concierge. English country-style home. Open year round. Seven rooms with private and shared baths. Rates: $50 single, $65 double, including Continental breakfast. No liquor served, guests may bring their own. Children under 6 free. Well-behaved pets welcome. Visa, MasterCard, American Express accepted. Additional Boulder activities include University of Colorado cultural events, a Shakespeare festival, and Chautauqua Society seasonal programs.

DIRECTIONS: From Denver on US 36 to Arapahoe Ave. and turn left toward mountains. Proceed to corner of Arapahoe and 22nd St.

A wonderful family of innkeepers

From the minute you arrive at The Peck House you begin to understand why, soon after their honeymoon here, Gary and Sally St. Clair bought the place. Snatches of Chopin and Mozart envelop you on the long porch of this red and white frame building, once a stop on the stagecoach route and now the oldest operating hotel in Colorado.

The music originates in the bar, where two oversize windows reveal craggy peak upon peak of the eastern slope of the Rockies.

In the many-windowed dining room, candles and fresh sprigs of flowers add snippets of light and color to the room's deep red cloths and carpeting. A dinner menu offering trout stuffed with cornbread, baby shrimp and mushrooms, and beef and oyster pie contrasts with a Champagne brunch on Sunday offering trout or quail with eggs. A gourmet picnic basket can be arranged that includes Dungeness crab, paté, and wine for hikers exploring the wildflower-rich countryside. Gary's teenage children do a lot of the amazing cooking, while he, a restaurateur, supervises everything.

The lodgings are pleasing too. For example, the Governor's Quarters, a guest room on the first floor, is cranberry papered and still has the beautiful wainscotting installed by Peck's son. An Eastlake mirrored secretary, a high-back walnut headboard, and a red velvet setee add to the effect.

It is apparent that the Peck House is the St. Clair family's new love, just as it was James Peck's when he built it in 1862, after laying claim to one of Empire's best gold mines.

THE PECK HOUSE, P.O. Box 428, Empire, CO 80438; (303) 569-9870; Gary and Sally St. Clair, Innkeepers. Original stagecoach house and oldest operating hotel in Colorado. Open year round. Ten rooms, private and shared baths. Rates: $25 to $50 single and double; 2 room suite $60. Dining room serves lunch and dinner. Bar open. Children welcome. No pets. Visa, MasterCard, American Express, Diners Club, Carte Blanche accepted. Nearby there is hiking, horseback riding, fishing, and a silver mine, steam train, and museum in historic Georgetown.

DIRECTIONS: From Denver drive on I-70 west to US 40, follow 2 miles to Empire to large building on right of highway, sign visible.

The St. Clair family: Gary, Sally, Mary, Mike, and Michele.

Green Mountain Falls OUTLOOK LODGE COLORADO

In a small town with lots to do

This 1881 parsonage-turned-inn was used by vacationing Congregational ministers, so it is not surprising to find the church they attended next door. Reputed to be furnished with original parsonage furniture, the inn has turn-of-the-century pieces that are charming but far from elegant. Four bedrooms in the original inn are complemented by an additional eight in the summer annex, most furnished with oak chests and painted iron or wooden bedsteads covered with patchwork patterned coverlets.

Impy Ahern, the affable innkeeper, provides all the conveniences of home to her family of guests. She is happy to have them fry up a day's catch in her inviting kitchen and she keeps a separate refrigerator for storing their food. For baby there is a pressed-wood high chair, and there are boxes of toys for the kids. Shoes left outside your room at night appear shined the next day.

The town of Green Mountain Falls offers vacationing guests many activities at no extra charge. There are hiking trails and bridle paths, a trout-stocked lake, and a swimming pool, tennis courts, volleyball, and a community hall that has bingo games during the week and dances on Saturday night. All of these are a short walk from the inn.

It is easy to see why ministers came to this mountain inn to find spiritual solace.

"I will lift up mine eyes unto the hills from whence cometh my help. . ."

That same inspiration and beauty will delight the inngoer today.

OUTLOOK LODGE, Box 5, Green Mountain Falls, CO 80819; (303) 684-2303; Impy Ahern, Innkeeper. Former parsonage overlooking Alpine village. Twelve rooms with private and shared baths. Rates: $23 to $28 single, $25 to $32 double including Continental breakfast. No restaurant or bar on premises. Guests may bring own liquor. Children and pets welcome. Visa and MasterCard accepted. Nearby recreation includes skiing, Garden of the Gods, cog railway, trout fishing, Cheyenne Mountain Zoo.

DIRECTIONS: From Denver on I-25 south to Colorado Springs. Take Pikes Peak exit which becomes US 24 west to Green Mountain Falls exit. Follow left curve in road into town and drive around lake to parking lot next to church. Flight of steps leads up to inn. To avoid steps look for road at side of parking lot leading up to inn.

The inn, once the parsonage of the Little Church in the Wilderness.

Bed down like guests did a century ago

In the 1880s water brought people to the Jackson Hotel—to the Poncha mineral hot springs. It is still water that keeps them coming today, but now it is the Arkansas River and the excitement of navigating a raft past breathtaking scenery through pulsating white water.

The Jackson Hotel is still a good place to stay—its fortunes have changed for the better since Bruce and Marla Solper bought it four years ago. After decades of neglect, the old hotel is being restored with partner Glenn Sheppard's help. Some of its original furnishings have been brought down from the attic and returned to guest rooms that Jesse James, Susan B. Anthony, and Rudyard Kipling once stayed in.

The dining room is a plus. It serves three meals a day in the summer and has a surprising menu. You can have Florentine crepes or cheese blintzes for breakfast, and filet mignon or carbonnades à la flammande for dinner. The sour dough bread is not to be missed. Susan Bethany, manager and part owner, is the hotel's baker, and her breads and pastries are addictive.

In winter the old stone fireplace is ablaze for skiiers returning from Monarch. They bed down at the Jackson Hotel like guests did a century ago.

THE JACKSON HOTEL, 220 South Main St. P.O. Box 25, Poncha Springs, CO 81242; (303) 539-3122; Susan Bethany, Manager. Restored western clapboard rooming hotel. Open year round. Ten rooms including 2 suites use dormitory style mens' and womens' baths. Rates: $16 to $25. Restaurant serves 3 meals daily. Children under 6 free. No pets. Visa and MasterCard accepted. Nearby there are hot springs, white-water rafting, fishing, skiing, and kyaking.

DIRECTIONS: From Colorado Springs drive on Rte. 115 southwest about 25 miles to US 50 west for about 75 miles. Hotel is off highway in center of Poncha Springs on the right.

Manager Susan Bethany's drawing on the wall behind her anticipates the stove she wants for baking sour dough bread.

BLUE SKY INN

Where tranquility and beauty abound

During the short growing season in Buena Vista, the Blue Sky Inn's frontage is truly a Garden of Eden. Columbines, fuscia, lilacs, pansies, peonies, sweet William, and poppies are all ablaze. Although the gardens appear very casual, take note. They are all carefully planned, just as are the days of the innkeepers, Hazel and Bill Davis.

Hazel, who thrives on gardening, believes that seeds are planted in many ways; that all of life is planting and harvesting. Here not only the vegetables and flowers grow and flourish, so do the guests.

Bill's family belongings are well represented at the inn, particularly in the living room. There are two rosewood French parlor chairs, an ornately carved mahogany Italian desk, and a portrait of his great-great-grandfather, Robert Barnwell Rhett, a senator from Charleston who lost five sons to the Civil War. Persian rugs, belonging to Bill's father, add warmth and color. Upstairs, the bedrooms are finely appointed with well-cared-for mahogany period pieces and perhaps a velvet side chair or caned rocker—but always books.

Building is one of Bill's hobbies and his latest accomplishment would enhance the pages of an *Architectural Digest*. Next to the inn, he has recently completed an inspired mountain home that he and Hazel designed, complete with hothouse for growing their salad greens in winter. Here, fifteen miles east of the Continental Divide, the Davises plan and execute projects for a life that seems eternal.

BLUE SKY INN, 719 Arizona St., Buena Vista, CO 81211; (303) 395-8862; Hazel and Bill Davis, Innkeepers. Alpine style construction, built with Philippine mahogany. Open year round. Six rooms all with shared baths. Rates: $35 single, $45 double, including full breakfast. No bar or lounge but guests may bring own liquor. Children welcome. Pets allowed in outside pen. No credit cards accepted. Croquet, badminton, available at the inn. Nearby there is white-water rafting, ghost town trips, rockhounding, hiking, fishing, and skiing.

DIRECTIONS: From Denver US 285 southwest to Johnson Village. Take US 24 north 2 miles to Buena Vista. At US 24 and Main Street, go east on Main St. to Court St. Turn south on Court which becomes Arizona St. after 3 blocks. Continue to Blue Sky sign on the left side of the road.

The flower-filled gardens provide a colorful setting for the inn.

THE IMPERIAL HOTEL

Cripple Creek   **COLORADO**

A 14 carat gold tourist attraction

Dorothy Mackin believes that if you do something well and strive to keep quality high, profits will be the end result. She is right, but surprisingly enough, it is her guests that profit. The Imperial Hotel in Cripple Creek offers highly affordable turn-of-the-century rooms, a buffet table worthy of a city the size of New York, and an authentic melodrama performed by the hotel's own players.

Originally the Collins Hotel, the Imperial prospered from 1891 to 1903, during the gold boom. At one time it kept seven Pierce-Arrows for greeting the fifty-eight trains that arrived at the station daily.

As gold mining declined so did the hotel, and by 1946, when the Mackins bought it, it had been closed for two years and was bereft of furnishings. Slowly they began to renovate, a room at a time, always striving to maintain the feeling of the original era. Anxious to preserve Colorado's history, they salvaged what they could: furniture from the Antlers Hotel for their dining room, parts of the old First National Bank for a front desk, stained glass panels from the Glockner Sanitarium for dining room doors, and leaded glass fixtures for the lobby from the Pueblo County Court House. The Red Rooster lounge's mahogany and walnut bar is from the old Red Rooster Saloon in Twin Lakes.

A sumptuous buffet features hot entrées, enticing salads, and fresh vegetables. Helpful waiters, college students from all parts of the country, encourage returning for seconds and thirds. Wayne Mackin, a tireless host, often appears in the dining room ensuring that his guests are happy.

Dorothy Mackin, always interested and involved in theater, prides herself on having established the longest running melodrama theater in the United States. She selects and revises, for today's audiences, scripts which originally came west with the gold seekers. And she has authored a book on Melodrama Classics and how to stage them. Many of the Imperial's stars have gone on to greater heights: Ronnie Claire Edwards as a regular on the Waltons, Craig

Left: Above, a "command performance" of the Imperial Players with owners Wayne and Dorothy Mackin. *Below,* the Carlton Room, with the Golden Oak Bar and a mother-of-pearl inlaid grand piano.

One of several Victorian parlors.

Nelson in *Poltergeist,* folk singer Tom Paxton, and ragtime pianist Max Morath, whose piano, nicked by hurtled silver dollars, resides in one of the lounges.

A brochure in the lobby suggests reliving the era by driving to nearby ghost towns. The Imperial Hotel ensures that Cripple Creek will never become a ghost town.

THE IMPERIAL HOTEL, Box 247, Cripple Creek, CO 80813; (303) 689-2922; Dorothy and Wayne Mackin, Owners. Steve Hornibrook, Manager. Only hotel left that flourished when Cripple Creek was the world's largest gold camp. Open mid-May to mid-October. Twenty-five rooms with private and shared baths. Rates: $18 to $24 single, $25 to $30 double; other accommodations available off premises. Dining room serves 3 meals daily, buffet style. There are 4 cocktail lounges. Children welcome. No pets. Visa, MasterCard, American Express accepted. Recreational facilities include hotel theater, and nearby Cripple Creek narrow gauge railroad, museum, underground tours of gold mines, ghost towns, camping.

DIRECTIONS: From Denver I-25 south to Colorado Springs. Take US 24 west to town of Divide, and Rte. 67 south to Cripple Creek.

A marvelous inn with incredible innkeepers

This Colorado Springs inn is fast becoming a legend, like Pikes Peak, which soars behind it. The legend is the making of two Dallas women, Dot Williams and Ruth Williams, who came to Colorado Springs and got William Thomas Odum, an inspired Dallas architect, to help them. Anxious to preserve an historical site, and determined to give the city a proper inn, the women were undaunted by their inability to get backing from ten banks or the clearance they needed from the city.

Good triumphed in the end. In 1977 the Small Business Administration came through with a loan and variance proceedings led to an agreement.

The exterior of the house was totally restored and trimmed in vibrant magenta, lavender, and brick-red orange to emphasize its handsome structural lines. Rooms which had deteriorated into tiny run-down apartments were converted into fourteen guest rooms. The 1955 Goodwill furniture was sold at a lawn sale, and Victorian era furnishings were bought on a three week shopping spree through Iowa, Illinois, Michigan, and Kansas. Wonderful breakfasts were planned that include fresh fruit, homemade breads, and baked eggs or quiche. Soon no trace was left of the inn's former state, nor of the former occupant who would ride his Harley Davidson up the staircase at night and park it outside his door. At last Colorado Springs had a proper country inn!

In January, 1982, the innkeepers purchased the building next door, a sprawling turn-of-the-century sanitarium. Zoned for replacement by a high rise building, the innkeepers were determined to save it, and, above all, to protect the site of their beloved inn. This imposing house is now an addition to the Hearthstone, with the original carriage house connecting the two. Used as a lounge, the carriage house is furnished with writing desks, comfortable chairs, and an old fashioned pump organ. The sanitarium

"Visibly hearty and appealing colors" were used by the architect to highlight the building.

now boasts ten charming guest rooms, and a three story stair-tower constructed with glass panels that offer a stunning view of Pikes Peak.

In 1858, when gold was discovered not far from here, prospectors scrambled out west to stake their claim. It was "Pikes Peaks or Bust." Many of the tenderfoot miners went bust but the hardier ones stuck it out and got rich. Successful prospectors, Dot Williams and Ruth Williams have staked their claim here.

THE HEARTHSTONE INN, 506 North Cascade, Colorado Springs, CO 80903; (303) 473-4913; Dot Williams and Ruth Williams, Innkeepers. An 1885 mansion connected to newly restored adjoining building. Open year round. Twenty-six rooms, most with private bath. Rates: $40 to $70 single, $48 to $75 double, including full breakfast. No bar, guests may bring own liquor. Children and pets welcome. Visa and MasterCard accepted. Pikes Peak, Garden of the Gods, Cave of the Winds, skiing, U.S. Air Force Academy are all nearby.

DIRECTIONS: From Denver I-25 south to exit 143, Unitah St. Travel east to 3rd stoplight. Turn right on Cascade Ave. for 7 blocks. The inn will be on the right at the corner of St. Vrain and Cascade.

The Library guest room, warmed by its uniquely-cased and tiled fireplace.

THE BALLOON RANCH

Del Norte   **COLORADO**

2000 foot thrills and exotic cooking

The thrill of soaring aloft in a hot air balloon makes you wonder why this is America's only balloon resort. The quietness and tranquility are becalming as you float above the landscape and ponder the undulating mountains that surround this valley, the snaking creek, and the planted alfalfa and barley fields that appear like a painting below.

Every morning at five-thirty, weather permitting, the balloonists meet for coffee, muffins, and take-off. The largest balloon holds six people and usually ascends about two thousand feet. Traveling at the same speed as the wind, the balloon is controlled vertically, varying its altitude to pick up alternate currents. Radio contact is maintained with the ground crew, who meet the balloonists when conditions are right for landing.

Landing usually takes place in the corner of a field in the San Luis Valley surrounding the ranch. A bottle of Champagne, traditionally brought to the landing site to assuage any irate farmers, will be uncorked and sipped by chasers, pilot and crew, who then return to the dining room for a hearty breakfast.

The chef at this ranch is special. Formerly the owner of Arno's in Houston, Michael Stein has garnered many awards. Some of his specialties at the ranch include duck with black currant sauce, shrimp Lyon Dijonaise, whole baked trout in cucumber sauce, and endless fresh pasta dishes. There is even lox on the menu and "the best bagels we can get out here in the wilderness."

The Balloon Ranch is currently being managed by Roger and Kathy Humbke, and its handsomely rustic, two-story pine lodge, is furnished in handcrafted furniture. A soaring beamed ceiling marks its interior, as well as a large stone fireplace, a dining area, a usually-open bar, and eight comfortable bedrooms off the balcony. Indian designs on chair fabrics and bedspreads add western warmth, to the whole.

Three deluxe pine cabins, some with fireplaces and one with a kitchen facility and wood-burning stove,

are scattered beyond the lodge for guests desiring more privacy.

Pilots David Levin and Alan Postelnek are very experienced, and easily win the trust and confidence of first-time balloonists. They look forward to taking up novices because "they always react so favorably." Are you ready for launching? Up, up, and away!

THE BALLOON RANCH at San Luis Valley, Star Route, Box 41, Del Norte, CO 81132; (303) 754-2533; Roger and Kathy Humbke, Managers. Eight room Alpine lodge with 6 shared baths and 6 rooms in 3 cabins with baths. Open Memorial Day through end of November. Rates: $95 to $165 single, $170 to $270 double, daily; $570 to $990 single, $1020 to $1620 double, weekly. All meals included. Bar. Ballooning extra. 15% service charge additional. Children welcome. Pets not encouraged. Visa, MasterCard, American Express accepted. Hot air ballooning, tennis, swimming pool, hot tub, sauna, horseback riding on premises. Nearby are ghost towns, Cumbres and Toltec scenic railroad, skiing, geological attractions.

DIRECTIONS: From Denver US 285 southwest 190 miles to Del Norte. Rte. 112 northeast 3 miles to La Garita turn off. North for 7 miles, turn left at Balloon Ranch sign and go 1 mile. Also from Denver and Albuquerque, Frontier and Rocky Mountain airlines fly to Alamosa airport 45 miles from ranch. Pickup at nominal fee.

Left: Seconds after lift-off on the maiden voyage of the balloon designed by ranch's pilot David Levin. It was also the maiden voyage of all three passengers: Fred Busk and Terry Berger flanking ranch manager's wife Kathy Humbke.
OVERLEAF: Dawn's early light illuminates Balloon Ranch and the San Luis Valley, an ideal area for hot air ballooning.

STRATER HOTEL

Durango   **COLORADO**

Where the old days become the "good old days"

Dating back a century, The Strater Hotel is located in Durango, a town created by the Denver and Rio Grande Railroad. People from all over the world come here to ride the narrow guage train from Durango to Silverton, a spectacular forty-five mile ride through the Animas River Canyon and Gorge.

The Strater Hotel attracts people too. Built by twenty-year-old Henry Strater, it is now owned and managed by Earl Barker and his wife, Jentra. They have turned the old days into the "good old days." You can sleep on a half tester bed recovered from a Vicksburg mansion, yet still have up-to-date plumbing and room service via a bedside phone. Flocked wallpapers, heavy velvet draperies, fretwork, and marble topped pieces bring back the Victorian era, but modern conveniences make that era easy to enjoy.

Dining, too, is easy to enjoy here. The Columbian Room is the more formal of the two dining rooms. Though it replaced an old barber shop, it is elegant, with green velvet draperies, mirrored walls, and framed Victorian nudes behind the bar. The more casual Opera House, formerly part of a theater, has its original brick southwest wall. Stained glass windows radiate scattered light. Both dining rooms share the same menu, and prime ribs or fresh sea food are good bets for dinner. Chilled wine glasses and rolling salad and dessert carts are standard fare and service is always pleasant and gracious.

The Diamond Belle, a "Gay 90s Saloon," has a mahogany bar complete with bullet hole from a bar room fight. Gold fringed, red velvet drapes set the stage for mustachioed bartenders and scantily attired barmaids, and songs of a by-gone-era are hammered out daily on a honky tonk piano, for locals and tourists.

From June to September, the Diamond Circle Theater features turn-of-the-century melodramas staged in a cabaret setting. Orvis Grout, former director of

Left: The hotel built by twenty-year-old Henry Strater, who overcame three handicaps: no money, no hotel experience, and, being a minor, no right to make legal contracts. His one advantage was the cost of bricks: $4.50 a thousand in 1887 as against $200 a thousand today. OVERLEAF: The Durango and Silverton narrow gauge railroad skirting the Animus River canyon—the treacherous gorge of the River of Lost Souls.

The lobby typifies the hotel's furnishings—Victoriana thriving in a western setting.

the Civic Theater in Colorado Springs, is responsible for its finesse. The cast serves drinks to guests during intermission, and a lively olio, or medley of musical pieces, is presented after the show.

Operating in the same spirit as the Durango to Silverton train, the Strater Hotel presents authentic local history combined with up-to-date service.

STRATER HOTEL, 699 Main St., Durango, CO 81301; (303) 247-4431. Earl Barker, Manager. An ornate 1887 brick hotel with all modern conveniences. Open year round. 94 rooms with private baths. Rates: $35 to $45 single, $45 to $50 double. Off-season rates available mid-Oct. through mid-May. Two restaurants open daily for all meals. Children welcome. No pets. Visa, MasterCard, Diners Club, American Express, Carte Blanche accepted. Melodrama theater in hotel; Durango and Silverton Narrow Gauge Railroad in town; Mesa Verde National Park, San Juan National Forest and skiing in area.

DIRECTIONS: From Denver US 285 south to Monte Vista. Take US 160 west to Durango. Go to second stop light, turn right, proceed to first light and take left. Hotel is up block on left.

European ambience, Yankee spirit

About seven years ago, when he was a guide for American cyclists and mountain climbers in Switzerland, Tom Galbraith read, in the *Rocky Mountain Gazette,* about Silverton, Colorado. Wanting to come back to America, he came to this small Rocky Mountain town where he could mountain climb and ski and contribute to the community. His contribution to Silverton is "a very reasonable trip into the past."

When it comes to lodging, don't expect first class accommodations, just charm. The rooms have interesting period furniture, but they are still being restored. There are water stains on the foyer wallpaper from the roof which used to leak, and the European-style bathroom accommodations are scant, but things are slowly improving. For the past six years Galbraith has been pouring all of his love for the place, his energy, his profits, into restoring the building, whose ground floor was a French bakery, the upstairs a fashionable boarding place.

The restaurant, along with a charming Victorian dining room, offers wonderful omelets for breakfast, including the French Bakery omelet prepared from cheddar cheese, salsa, mushrooms, and sour cream. Lunches can be mouth-watering soup or salad, and there is a buffet where sandwiches are made to order. A variety of char-broiled steaks, as well as fish and fowl, are available for dinner.

In time this lodging and restaurant will be the most charming and sought after in town. It's beginning to be that already.

THE FRENCH BAKERY RESTAURANT AND TELLER HOUSE HOTEL, 1250 Greene St., Silverton, CO 81433; (303) 387-5423; Tom Galbraith, Innkeeper. A two-story masonry building, circa 1885, with a restaurant on lower floor and pension above. Open year round. Ten rooms share 2 baths. Rates: $18 single, $24 double, including breakfast. Special rates for American Youth Hostel members. Restaurant serves 3 meals Thursday through Monday; breakfast and lunch only, other days. Children welcome. Pets welcome if well behaved. Visa, MasterCard, American Express accepted. Walking tour of historic Silverton, hiking, skiing, fishing, and Durango and Silverton railroad are some of the recreation facilities available nearby.

DIRECTIONS: From Denver I-70 west to Grand Junction, take US 550 south to Silverton. Hotel is in center of town.

Tom Galbraith in his French Bakery Restaurant, downstairs from the Teller House.

ALMA HOUSE

End of the line for narrow gauge train buffs

Don Stott, president of Silverton's Chamber of Commerce, stands facing the Alma House.

Don Stott's romance with Silverton began when he was eighteen years old and came out from Washington, D.C. to ride the Durango and Silverton narrow gauge railroad. Always a train nut, Don ended up years later buying the Grand Imperial Hotel in Silverton.

After selling the Grand Imperial for a tidy profit and operating a restaurant in Phoenix, Arizona, Don has returned to Silverton. Homesick for the train, and the pine-and-aspen-covered San Juan Mountains that surround this small mining town, Don is now operating The Alma House for non-smokers.

Comfortable rooms, all with views of the towering mountains, offer queen-size beds, individual thermostats, Don's own photos of old trains and trolleys, and color TV's which play classic films from Stott's own video library every night. Right after New Year's The Alma House features a thirteen-weekend film festival. For a room for two, including meals and six features, the weekend is a bargain at $100.00.

On railroad tracks outside The Alma is a parlor observation car—Don's dream-come-true. Built in the 1890s, it ran on the Great Northern's crack Oriental Express between Chicago and Seattle. It has been converted into two oak paneled, sumptuously furnished Victorian guest rooms, each with private bath, and affords the ultimate bed and breakfast accommodations to train nuts the world over.

THE ALMA HOUSE, 220 East 10th St., Silverton, CO 81433; (303) 387-5336. Don and Jolene Stott. Restored 1898 stone and frame European-style hotel for non-smokers only. Open year round. Ten rooms including 2 rooms in restored railroad observation car. Shared baths. Rates: $25 single, $30 double, including Continental breakfast. No restaurant or bar, guests may bring own liquor. No charge for children with sleeping bags. Pets allowed. Visa, MasterCard, American Express accepted. Nearby recreation includes the Durango and Silverton railroad, hiking, fishing.

DIRECTIONS: From Denver I-70 west to Grand Junction to US 550 south to Silverton. Turn left onto Greene St. for about ½ mile, make right at Plateau gas station for 1 block.

Historic Silverton's main street. On left is Grand Imperial Hotel, now being restored.

NEW SHERIDAN HOTEL

Telluride   **COLORADO**

The main street of Telluride.

Where culture reaches new heights

In the 1870s, when the Indians left Telluride, legend says they put a curse on the place. The curse seems to have lifted and Telluride is now emerging for a variety of reasons. The New Sheridan Hotel is one of them.

Built in 1895, the hotel became the center of Telluride's high society during the Gilded Age. William Jennings Bryan, Colorado's choice for president, stayed here, and a lavish suite still bears his name. Recently, after years of decline, the hotel has been restored by Walter McClennan, the new owner, who leases out its historic restaurant, theater, and bar to specialists.

Jim Russell's Sheridan Bar is for locals and guests alike. It is relaxed and well worn but has elegant features, like its mahogany back bar. Clocked at 111.29 miles per hour, bartender Marti Kuntz is the world's fastest woman skier.

Julian's, the restaurant, is captivating in every sense, and its cocktail lounge, a mixture of rust walls with floral and nude découpage, plum carpeting, and oversized leaded etched-glass lantern chandeliers, is sheer beauty. Twentieth Century Fox created the walls when they filmed *Butch and Sundance: The Early Days* here in 1978. Run by Wayne and Elizabeth Gustafson, it specializes in Northern Italian cuisine.

Finally there is the Sheridan Opera House, run by former Janis Films executive Bill Pence and his wife Stella. Along with manager Jim Bedford, they have put together a program of classic and up-to-the minute movies that would distinguish a theater in any of the world's largest cities. The Telluride Film Festival, held over Labor Day weekend, has become second in importance only to Cannes. Annually honoring three greats from the industry, recipients have included Robert Altman, Jack Nicholson, and Francis Ford Coppola. *Napoleon* was shown here before it played in New York, and film maker Abel Gance flew over from Paris to view it.

Views of the ski slopes are everywhere. Twenty-three miles of world-class trails range from the awesome Plunge and Spiral Stairs to some of the choicest beginners' terrain. The ski lift in town makes the mountain accessible to anyone.

This town of 1,000 residents supports and runs KOTO FM, a non-profit radio station that features sixty volunteer disc jockeys as well as innumerable talk shows. A Blue Grass Festival, a Dance Festival, and a Chamber Music Festival are held annually. High in the Rocky Mountains, Telluride is not only prospering, people say it is the up-and-coming Aspen. And the New Sheridan Hotel is helping it happen.

THE NEW SHERIDAN HOTEL, 231 Colorado Ave., Telluride, CO 81435; (303) 728-4351; Sue Paasche, Manager. Newly restored Victorian hotel and still the center of Telluride society. Open year round. Thirty rooms, half with a view of the San Juan Mountains. Rates: $30 to $56. Private and European-style shared baths. Three meals served daily in restaurant. Bar and lounge. One child under 12 free. No pets. Visa, MasterCard, American Express accepted. Hotel Opera House has yearly film festival and daily films. Annual jazz, dance, and music festivals in town. Nearby skiing, tennis, horseback riding, hiking, hang gliding, fishing.

DIRECTIONS: From Denver I-70 west to Grand Junction. Take US 50 south to Montrose to US 550 south to Ridgeway to 62 west to Placerville to Rte. 145 south to Telluride. Hotel is 4 blocks down on left side.

Left: The Opera House, *above,* showing John Ericksen's handpainted screen from 1914. *Below,* the cocktail lounge, whose walls were decorated by Twentieth Century Fox.

Fine food, art, and live entertainment

The St. Elmo Hotel is unique! With only eleven guest rooms, it features services befitting a resort. In addition to attractively furnished Victorian-style rooms, it has an art gallery, a restaurant, and live entertainment.

Throughout the summer, entertainers appear daily on the hotel's patio, the original site of Kitty Heit's turn-of-the-century Bon Ton restaurant. Here lunch is served under colorful umbrellas, against snow-peaked mountains. Entertainment ranges from a guitar and fiddle duo, like the Bonney Brothers, to the totally unexpected: juggling, belly dancing, and a hayride through town accompanied by guitar and fiddle.

Run by chef-owner Chuck Norton, the Bon Ton Restaurant is now safely tucked away in the hotel's basement. Cypress wainscotting brought from Chuck's native New Orleans complements Williamsburg blue booths partitioned by etched-glass panels. The Italian

Left: Half-tester, carved walnut bed with peach silk lining in the Bridal Suite.

cuisine is excellent but there are other things not to be missed like the individual beef Wellingtons, steak with a wine, soy, and ginger sauce, and "La Dolce Vita", a delectable walnut pie.

The art gallery is the brainchild of Chuck's wife Sue. Featuring outstanding local artists, it offers a pleasing selection of pottery, paintings, photographs, jewelry, and Sue's own weavings.

Originally a lodging for the miners in this community, the hotel was closed for a period of time. It resurfaced during the forties when it was won in a poker game. Bought three years ago by the Nortons and their partners, the Koshes, it has been restored and lovingly refurbished.

ST. ELMO HOTEL, 426 Main St., Ouray, CO 81427; (303) 325-4318; Chuck and Sue Norton, Innkeepers. Queen Anne-style hotel built at the turn of the century. Open year round. Seven rooms with shared baths and 4 suites with private baths. Rates: $18 to $48, including Continental breakfast. Restaurant serves 2 meals daily. Children welcome. No pets. Visa and MasterCard accepted. On premises, live-entertainment all summer, sauna and art gallery. Nearby, horseback riding, rafting, hot springs, sledding, cross-country skiing, and jeep trips into the San Juan mountains.

DIRECTIONS: From Denver I-70 west to Grand Junction. US 550 south to Ouray. Hotel is on right side, 5 blocks down.

In summer, the patio features live entertainment

A country inn that's good for you

This is a place for all seasons. Located in Ouray, the "Switzerland of America," and built over hot springs, the Wiesbaden has a school for cross-country skiing and three hot-spring pools for inngoers to soak in.

The most exotic place to soak is in a cave under the lodge, where hot springs were discovered by miners digging for gold at the turn of the century. Here you lie deep in the steamy depths of the mountain, in mineral-rich one hundred and six degree water. In winter, steam rises from the outdoor pool to the top of the lodge, and guests alternate between lying in the snow and swimming.

Après le soak, Sam, the masseur, and Liz, the masseuse, apply Swedish and accupressure massage. Sam offers tips for curing aches and pains, and claims

Left: the hot-springs pool, the main lodge, and the ever-present San Juan mountains.

sweating rids the body of toxins. Invigorating salt rubs and herbal mud-pac facials are popular too.

Increasingly touted by those who have been here, this European-style lodge has surprisingly attractive rooms. Mary Linda and Bill Poehnert have refurbished them with colorful and interesting wall papers, quilts, and period furnishings. The sitting room in the lodge, looking out on snow-capped mountains, is comfortable and inviting. Its wood-burning stove is the only heater here; the other rooms are warmed by the springs.

WIESBADEN HOT SPRINGS SPA AND LODGINGS, Box 349, Ouray, CO 81427; (303) 325-4347; Mary Linda and Bill Poehnert, Innkeepers. Alpine style cedar chalet with guest lodgings. Open year round. Fifteen rooms including 3 suites, all with private bath. Rates: $41 to $58. No restaurant or bar, guests may bring own liquor. Children welcome. No pets. Visa and MasterCard accepted.

Facilities include hot springs, pool, vapor cave, sauna, exercise rooms, salt rubs, facials, and massages. Nearby horseback riding, rafting, sledding, cross-country skiing.

DIRECTIONS: From Denver I-70 west to Grand Junction. US 550 south to Ouray. Drive down main street about 3 blocks and turn left at bank. Go up hill for two blocks until road ends.

The mountain, showing behind the fireplace, is the conversation piece in this unusual guest room.

In her hogan, Navajo weaver Suzie Yazzie demonstrates the art of rug making for tourists to Utah's Monument Valley.

Left: Mesa Verde, in southwest Colorado, is an ancient Indian cliff palace of 223 rooms abandoned in 1300 A.D. during a twenty-year drought. It was discovered in 1886 by two cowboys, Richard Wetherill and Charles Mason, and was established as a national park by an act of Congress in 1906.

OVERLEAF: the monumental Monument Valley.

RECAPTURE LODGE

Where you learn to love Monument Valley

The world here is revealed without searching; there are no secrets. A lunar-like landscape of red-tinged bluffs and river-valley cliffs surrounds the lodge. The houses of Mormon pioneers still stand here in southern Utah's first Mormon settlement.

Gene and Mary Foushee's lodge is not for everyone. There are no Victorian furnishings and no Continental breakfasts; just motel-type furniture and knotty pine. But the guest rooms are comfortable, there is a solar heated pool, and a pine-paneled room where Gene shows slides. The laundry on the premises is the only one operating from here to Arizona. Of the two cafes in this town of two hundred and fifty people, one serves Indian stew and frybread and is staffed by Navajo Indians.

During the day, Gene, a geologist and a naturalist, conducts tours in his four-wheel drive to prehistoric cliff dwellings, petroglyphs, and the 1880 Mormon Trail. His love of this geological oasis is infectious. A full day tour of Monument Valley is a must and always includes a visit to a Navajo hogan where lunch is prepared by an Indian family.

Gene has planted trees for the Navajo family he visits—a cottonwood, currant, black locust, pine, and North Carolina poplar. Every time he comes, he brings water from town for the Indians and trees, for there is none in this arid desert. When he tells you his dream is to bring Leonard Bernstein to the Navajo Indians, you can understand why fans return year after year to "recapture" their experience here.

RECAPTURE LODGE, Box 36, Bluff, UT 84512; (801) 672-2281. Gene and Mary Foushee. Open year round. Spruce and ponderosa pine lodge built by the Foushees. Seventeen rooms with private baths. Rates: $18 to $25 single, $22 to $35 double. Additional accommodations available off premises. No meals served. Children and pets welcome. Visa and MasterCard accepted. Facilities include heated pool, croquet, basketball, horseshoes. Tours of Monument Valley and southeast Utah from beginning of April to end of October.

DIRECTIONS: 130 miles from Denver. Take I-70 southwest to Crescent Junction (Utah), and US 191 south through Canyonland region to Bluff.

The Lodge, entirely built by geologist-owner Gene Foushee.

Monument Valley GOULDING'S LODGE UTAH

The scene of many Western movies

Located in Monument Valley, and surrounded by Navajo land, Goulding's Lodge looks out on a set only God could have built. Harry Goulding, a Colorado cowboy, came upon the desolate, haunting beauty of its soaring spires, its buttes, its mesas, its arches, back in 1921. It was love at first sight, and before the area was made a reservation, Goulding managed to buy one square mile of this awesome terrain. With stone quarried here, Goulding built a trading post at the base of Tsay-Kizzi-Mesa, where, from their front porch, Harry and his wife Mike looked out on a museum of monumental earth sculpture.

John Ford put Monument Valley on the map in 1938 when Goulding convinced him to shoot *Stage Coach* there. Harry had gone to Hollywood, armed with pictures of his beloved valley, and managed to convince the movie moguls it was the perfect setting. The Indians got a chance to work in the movies, and their medicine man was put at the top of the payroll to make sure the weather was right for shooting.

Navajo guides conduct tours of the valley, including a twilight tour when the mood is intensely romantic and the shimmering colors of the monuments are most magnificent.

Harry believed that one day people from all over the world would come to Monument Valley. The people have come, but Harry has met his maker, and guests who stayed here back when say the charisma he brought to the lodge is no longer here. Neither are the ranch-style meals. But the awesome beauty of the monumental red-rock fantasies is untouched and that is reason enough to come. Again and again.

GOULDING'S LODGE, P.O. Box 1, Monument Valley, UT 84536; (801) 727-3231; Gerald Lafont, Manager. Open March 15 to November. Nineteen rooms with private baths. Rates: $40 single and double; 2 cabins available. Three meals daily in dining room. No bar, guests may bring own liquor. Children welcome. Pets on leash. Visa and MasterCard accepted. Curio shop on premises selling Indian crafts.

DIRECTIONS: From Las Vegas US 93 south to Kingman; I-40 east to Flagstaff; US 89 north to Junction US 160; east to Kayenta; US 163 north to Utah-Arizona border, turn left at county road to Goulding's 2 miles.

View of Monument Valley from the dining room, which starred in one of John Ford's movies.

BRIGHAM STREET INN

Salt Lake City

UTAH

Impeccable taste in a great new inn

If Bloomingdale's owned and managed an inn, this would be it. It is the showplace of the West, an elegant bed and breakfast, abounding in works of art and rooms that feature a dozen designers' concepts.

Born of the 1898 Walter C. Lyne House, this red sandstone and brick three-story Victorian building has been restored and remodeled by John Pace, its architect-innkeeper. Fireplaces, bedrooms, and baths were added, storage space created, and a cooling system installed throughout. All this, along with impeccable furnishing, was accomplished over a five-month period and came as a surprise to the Paces.

Nancy Pace, John's wife and co-innkeeper, came upon the house when she chaired the Utah Heritage Foundation's Designers Showcase in 1982. Selecting a site for this fund raiser was just the beginning. The Paces were so taken with the house they bought it, and after restoration, furnishing, and the fund-raising event were over, they became bona fide innkeepers. No one is more qualified. They are both concerned with quality and attention to detail, and both business persons and visitors will find their needs being met; almost anything can be arranged here by the caring and capable staff.

Utah's leading interior designers have created diverse and beautiful rooms, and tours are still being conducted through its splendid interior. The foyer's original oak wainscotting and staircase, and the bird's-eye maple fireplace in the parlor, are merely a beginning. The old Tibetan tapestry in the formal dining room, and the horsehair porter's chair and Steinway grand in the parlor, add unanticipated drama, while upstairs each guest room vies for

Left and above: Room seven typifies the exquisite detailing found throughout the inn.

attention. Victorian revival and American Federal, classic eighteenth century, Country, Oriental, and Art Nouveau, circa Hector Guimard, are all periods on display. The "cellar space" is casual elegance; a town house suite with living room, bedroom, kitchen, double whirlpool bath, and private garden entrance.

In its infancy, this inn has already garnered awards for its owners in interior and architectural design. With such a variety of decor, there's a room for every taste and mood.

BRIGHAM STREET INN, 1135 East South Temple St., Salt Lake City, UT 84102; (801) 364-4461; John and Nancy Pace, Innkeepers. Victorian brick mansion built in 1898. Nine rooms, including 1 suite. Rates: $70 single, $85 double, suite $140, including Continental breakfast. No liquor served, guests may bring their own. Children welcome. No pets. Visa, MasterCard, American Express accepted. Temple Square, Salt Palace cultural center, Trolley Square. Prime ski areas at Snowbird and Alta within 45 minutes.

DIRECTIONS: South Temple St. runs east and west from the Temple.

Right: Innkeeper-architect John Pace.

The elegant dining room, with its exquisite seventeenth-century Tibetan tapestry.

| Nephi | # THE WHITMORE | UTAH |

A place you have to see for yourself

This inn is a tribute to Mormon resourcefulness and industry. Don and Darline Bendoski spent three solid years refurbishing and restoring this jewel-like Victorian mansion from a building fronted by a used car lot to one of the most inventively and impeccably furnished inns to be found in any part of the country. Darline, a junkaholic since the age of ten, has furnished much of the inn with furniture which filled her eighteen room home, a garage, and a shed in her native California.

Between dinner courses, which she graciously serves in four richly-furnished dining rooms, guests wander around looking at her collections of old dishes, lace work, books, washstands, colorful bottles, and stoves (including a not-to-be-missed French blue porcelain stove, circa 1800). A white piano, a gilded armoire, a baby's bath tub, an old French ticket booth—all pop out of the most unlikely places. Even the philodendrons here repose in the unusual: they are planted on scales, in jugs, washstands, roasting pans, bottles, tea kettles, and bread tins.

"We hope you can keep eating as long as we bring out food." That can be a problem when there are seven courses. The entrée is usually prime ribs or chicken prepared with oranges or apricots. Wonderful homemade soup is served as well as salad, hot muffins with honey butter, and fudge or divinity as a final treat. The thing that will finally entice you away from the food is your room, guaranteed to have attractive eye-catching features, planned out to the most minute detail.

Innkeeper Darline Bendoski in front of the inn, a mansion built by banker George Whitmore in 1898.

The wood for the oak staircase, inlaid with burl fir, was imported from Europe.

In keeping with Mormon tradition, no smoking, coffe, tea, or alcohol are permitted here and Don thinks of the inn as a missionary tool. He sees it as an opportunity for guests to observe what two people who are sober, upright, and hardworking can accomplish. You leave here thinking hard—and amazed at what two people can do.

THE WHITMORE, 110 South Main St., Nephi, UT 84648; (801) 623-1200; Darline and Don Bendoski, Innkeepers. A Victorian mansion meticulously restored and decorated to perfection. Open year round. Ten rooms including 1 suite, all with private baths. Rates: $35 to $60. Breakfast extra on request. Dinner by reservation served Tuesday through Saturday. No smoking, no liquor, no coffee or tea served. No children or pets. Visa, MasterCard, Diners Club accepted. Old settlements at San Pete Valley, Salt Creek Canyon trout fishing, and Yuba Lake State Park. Skiing at nearby Provo.

DIRECTIONS: From Salt Lake City 88 miles south on I-15 into Nephi; down 10 blocks on right side.

A fine inn steeped in Mormon history

Each of the bedrooms in this inn is named after one of innkeeper Donna Curtis's polygamous great grandfather's wives: Melissa, Clarinda, Mary Ann, Sarah, Harriet, Susan, and Sarah Jane, all of whom he married between 1841 and 1857. The posterity accruing from these marriages is astounding, with just first wife Melissa's descendants numbering 4,903 in 1981.

Once private secretary and business agent to Mormon church founder Joseph Smith, Benjamin Johnson headed up a pioneering group to settle Salt Lake City. In addition to missions to Mexico and Canada, he carried the revelation on plural marriages to Hawaii in 1852. Years later, indicted for polygamy under the Edmunds-Tucker law, he successfully defended himself on the grounds that polygamy was practiced in the Old Testament by Abraham, Jacob, Moses, Solomon, and David. He also cited God's commandment to multiply and replenish the earth.

One of Benjamin's descendants, great granddaughter Donna Curtis, along with her husband Jay, have revived her family's colorful history in a gracious and charming country inn. Furnished in European and American period pieces, space is uncluttered and luxurious, and individual furnishings are prominent: a cerise velvet Victorian fainting couch, a carved walnut high-back bed, a carved oak armoire, a tin tub with oak molding, a quilt Jay's mother made at age thirteen.

The full breakfast, served in an elegant dining room, usually includes ham and eggs and a wonderful German pancake topped with apples, peaches, or strawberries. Brigham Young probably ate in this same dining room while his winter home was being built across the street (where Benjamin later wrote his memoirs).

Although situated in an out-of-the-way part of southwestern Utah, delectable fare and fascinating Mormon history are served up at the Seven Wives. It is well worth a visit.

SEVEN WIVES INN, 217 North 100 West, St. George, UT 84770; (801) 628-3737. Jay and Donna Curtis, Innkeepers. Southern Utah's first bed and breakfast, kitty corner from Brigham Young's winter home. Open year round. Eight rooms including 1 suite. Private and shared baths. Rates: $20 to $50 single or double, including full gourmet breakfast. No restaurant or bar, guests are welcome to bring own liquor. Children welcome. No pets. Visa, MasterCard, Diners Club, Carte Blanche accepted. Local recreation includes 4 golf courses, a Shakespeare Festival, and summer repertory theater. Zion and Bryce National Parks nearby.

DIRECTIONS: From Las Vegas 120 miles on I-15 to St. George. Take exit 6 (Bluff St.), follow for 1 mile to St. George Blvd. and turn right. Go 6 blocks to 100 West St., turn left for 1 block to inn. From Salt Lake City 330 miles on I-15 south to exit 8 (St. George Blvd.). West for 2 miles to 100 West Street, turn right 1 block.

Innkeepers Jay and Donna Curtis.

Room number one, named after first wife Melissa, is the most luxurious.

MIZPAH HOTEL

PHOTOGRAPHED BY GEORGE W. GARDNER

The jackpot in the desert

You come upon this oasis in the desert suddenly. There is no warning.

The Mizpah Hotel, between Las Vegas and Reno, is where Jack Dempsey worked as a bouncer, Howard Hughes married Jean Peters, and Bernard Baruch, advisor to presidents, became a stockholder in the company that built it.

Completed in 1908, with carpets of the "finest Brussels quality," the Mizpah became "the hotel" of Tonopah, befittingly grand for this silver-rich boom town. Constructed on the site of Jim Butler's original claim, today the hotel remains an elegant turn-of-the-century retreat, newly restored with fifty-six rooms

Left. The casino, where you win and lose in Victorian style.

and plenty of crystal, velvet, carved oak, purple-tinted windows, and reporcelained claw-foot tubs. There is a plush casino, and two posh restaurants open twenty-four hours a day, featuring good food at cheap, gaming-house prices.

There's money to be made here, and not only in "them thar hills." Claims are staked in the Mizpah's casino, at "21" and crap tables. "Slot machine" decor is rampant, and a progressive machine has been known to cough up eight thousand dollars for a lucky quarter. The Mizpah Hotel is the only place where you can gamble between Reno and Las Vegas, and it's said that Tonopah offers other pleasures as well.

The hotel was renovated by the Scott Corporation, owners of the Union Plaza Hotel in Las Vegas. It took four or five million dollars and was a labor of love. Frank Scott, chairman of the board, has been fond of the Mizpah since his days at Las Vegas High, when he stopped here en route to a sporting event. He has turned the Mizpah around, to reclaim its rightful place in Tonopah history.

Tonopah.

J. D. ADAMS

In 1908, when the hotel opened, the *Tonopah Bonanza* reported: "... should the guest desire, he can stroll into the office, state that he wants to be fed, bathed, and put to bed, and all these things will be attended to for him."

The Mizpah is still big on service.

MIZPAH HOTEL, 100 Main St., Tonopah, NV 89049; (702) 842-6202; Tom Newman, Manager. An elegantly restored 1907 hotel of 56 rooms with private baths, color TV, and individual thermostats. Open year round. Rates: $25 to $50 single. Restaurants include the Dempsey Room and the Pittman Room (open 24 hrs.). Bar in casino. No pets. MasterCard and American Express accepted. Live music and entertainment and gambling casino.

DIRECTIONS: Tonopah is mid-way between Reno and Las Vegas on US 95.

Right: The skylight transforms the brilliant desert sun into vibrant colors.

All the picture windows have been replaced with specially made stained glass etched with the Mizpah "M".

THE SAVAGE MANSION

Virginia City | NEVADA

PHOTOGRAPHED BY GEORGE W. GARDNER

The restoration is meticulous and complete.

A bonanza town comes back to life

In the mid-nineteenth century, Virginia City flourished as the silver capital of the West. The Comstock Lode alone produced close to a billion dollars in gold and silver, some of which helped to finance the Civil War. After the boom was over, the mining town lay untouched until a restoration movement revived it after World War II. You can still order a whiskey and water at the Bucket of Blood Saloon, visit the Piper's Opera House (where Lillian Russell and Lola Montez performed), see rows of cottages that belonged to ladies of pleasure, and tour fabulous mansions built by the Silver Kings.

The Savage Mansion is one of them. Built as a home for the superintendant of the Savage Mine, the top two floors served as the living quarters and the lower floor as mine and assay office. Many original items remain: a built-in eighteen-inch-thick vault to store bullion bars, a specimen case, telegraph equipment, and the mine's shift bell, which tolled three eight-hour shifts.

Left: The inn, *above,* overlooks the Savage mine. *Below,* the original mine office now displays mining artifacts.

The mansion's second floor is museum-like, with original period furnishings in the kitchen, parlor, and music room. It was from the balcony of this floor that U.S. Grant addressed the town when he came here to tour the mines. Grant's bedroom remains the same—the walnut high-back bed, the marble-top dresser, and the wicker chairs. Three additional bedrooms with charming original furnishings are on the third floor.

Directly across the way is the entrance to the mine, plunging three thousand feet into the core of Sun Mountain. Before closing, in 1895, the Savage Mine Company had hauled more than twenty million dollars in gold and silver out of Nevada's earth. Recently a new mine opened near the old Savage site. They're hauling up ore—and they're calling it the "New Savage Mine."

SAVAGE MANSION, 146 South D St., Virginia City, NV 89440; (702) 847-0574; Bob and Irene Kugler and Ann Louise Mertz, Innkeepers. Built in 1861 by the Savage Mine as office and residence, now restored as a 4 room inn. Open year round. Rates: $30 single, $40 double, including Continental breakfast. Master bedroom has half bath, others share. No bar, guests may bring own liquor. Children welcome. No pets. Visa and MasterCard accepted. Historic gold town with many attractions, including a restored Virginia and Truckee shortline railroad.

DIRECTIONS: From Reno US 395 south to Rte. 341 to Virginia City.

THE IDANHA HOTEL

A fine hotel restored to its former glory

This place was saved from urban renewal by Boisean Cal Jensen, a man who got tired of seeing his "childhood bulldozed away for parking lots." He and his White Savage Associates have bought and restored the historic Idanha Hotel.

No expense has been spared here, and the result is an elegant, classy affair. Extravagant touches include Alaskan marble, brass statue lamps, and an art deco chandelier from New York's old Astor Hotel. Guest rooms, newly enlarged, have been furnished in tasteful period decor, and the whole is in keeping with the French chateau-style architecture.

Personal touches abound. Beds are turned down, pillows fluffed each night, and babysitting and secretarial services are readily available. The hotel's vintage Packard or Rolls picks guests up at the airport.

Left: The 1948 Packard limousine parked in front of the hotel.

The popular bar here headlines a jazz combo which features pianist Gene Harris, who played with trumpet-great Miles Davis. Tables are set up around the group, and the atmosphere is relaxed and intimate. Musicians traveling through town pop in for impromptu jam sessions.

Peter Schott's restaurant off the lobby is elegant with its brass rails, lacy curtains, and Louis XIV wicker chairs. Formerly Sun Valley's head chef, Schott features Austrian Continental cuisine and an extensive wine list.

All this could have been lost to urban renewal.

IDANHA HOTEL, 10th and Main St., Boise, ID 83702; (208) 342-3611; Dana Freeland, Manager. French chateau-style building with 101 rooms and suites. Private and shared baths. Open year round. Rates: $25 to $70 single, $30 to $75 double, including Continental breakfast. Restaurant serves 2 meals 5 days a week; Saturday, dinner only is served. Children welcome. No pets. Visa, MasterCard, American Express, Diners Club accepted. Ski bus to Bogus Basin. Golf and tennis are available nearby. Sawtooth Mountains and recreation area within easy driving.

DIRECTIONS: Downtown Boise. City Center exit off I-84.

Peter Schott's Continental Restaurant features Austrian cuisine.

IDAHO CITY HOTEL

Idaho City   **IDAHO**

A town that won't let the past die

Don Campbell, owner of the hotel, was always fascinated with this gold mining town, where a lot of Idaho's history still exists. Since buying the hotel here in '74, he has spent seven years restoring it, weekends and nights. As the hard-working manager of Boise radio station KFXD, he finds working on the hotel the perfect antidote.

Located in the old Chinese section of town, this quaint old western "rooming-hotel" is simply furnished in oak period pieces. There is a public room

Left: The former newspaper office in the famous Idaho ghost town that refuses to die.

with a big oak table and easy chairs, and a gift shop selling local crafts. Other than the pop and candy machine, there is no food.

In 1865, Idaho City was the biggest and bawdiest gold mining camp west of the Mississippi. Twenty thousand people lived here. Today the three hundred inhabitants of this town refuse to let it die.

Preserved highlights include an early-day jail (built of hand-hewn timber and hand-wrought nails), the 1870 pioneer school, and the old newspaper office. The *Idaho World,* the state's oldest paper, is still being printed, and spans nearly a century of Boise Basin's history—as does the Idaho City Hotel.

THE IDAHO CITY HOTEL, Corner of Wallula and Montgomery St., Idaho City, ID 83631; (208) 392-4290. Vern and Tressa Baker, Managers. Restored old western rooming hotel. Open year round. Five rooms available. Rates: $18 single, $20 double. No meals or liquor, but guests may bring their own. Children welcome. Pets accepted. Visa and MasterCard accepted. Recreation facilities include picnic area and croquet. Nearby are natural hot springs, fishing, deer hunting, and Nordic skiing.

DIRECTIONS: From Boise drive North on Rte. 21, 35 miles to Idaho City.

ROCKY MOUNTAIN RANCH

Stanley   **IDAHO**

A fabulous ranch in steak-and-potatoes country

For three generations this ranch has been an ongoing family operation. Sisters Marisue and Mindee, daughters of owner Rozalys Smith, are now managing it. The girls, twenty-two and twenty-four, have been running the place for the last seven years.

Edmund Bogert, the girls' grandfather, bought the ranch in 1951, after Winston Paul, a Frigidaire distributor from New York, had the beautiful lodge and cabins constructed in 1930. All the logs were snaked off property north and east of the big meadow, and a crew of sixty men, including a blacksmith and stonemason, camped here and built the beautiful lodge-pole pine buildings. Complete with its own hydroelectric power plant, the ranch is now exactly as it was then—from the lodge and handcrafted cabins to the furnishings, trophies, and pictures on the walls. Even the original dining room chandeliers remain, light bulbs suspended from unusual twisted wood, made from trees that survive above the timberline.

This is real steak-and-potatoes country, and hearty gourmet food is served in the rustic dining room.

The inn at twilight, surrounded by purple sage.

Excellent tender steaks and chops are fired up by an outstanding chef. Baked Idaho potatoes are stuffed with real bacon bits, chives, butter and sour cream, and smothered with melted cheese. This and the garden-fresh vegetables, homemade salad dressings, breads and pastries baked on the premises (including a sinfully rich chocolate torte), draw people from Sun Valley, forty-five miles away. There is even an excellent local wine from the Ste. Chapelle Vineyards, outside of Boise.

From the front porch of the lodge, the Sawtooth Mountains tower above the valley, a magnified version of the Grand Tetons. Jagged snow-capped peaks cast their shadows on Alpine pastures covered with glorious profusions of sego lilies, violet lupins, and Indian paintbrush. Natural hot springs proliferate and it is not unusual to see a fisherman sitting in a hot spring, casting for trout in the Salmon River that runs through the property.

Quiet, relaxed, private, and peaceful, this beautiful ranch maintains its traditions from one generation to the next.

All the furniture was handmade on the ranch.

Left: Owner Rozalys Smith behind the ranch's rustic check-in desk. OVERLEAF: The picture postcard ranch setting.

IDAHO ROCKY MOUNTAIN RANCH, Stanley, ID 83278; (208) 774-3544; Rozalys Bogert Smith, Owner; Marisue and Mindee Smith, Managers. Guest ranch with spectacular view of Sawtooth Mountains. Open mid-June to Labor Day. Five rooms in lodge with baths; 13 cabins with baths or showers. Rates: $32 single, $36 to $45 double. Breakfast and dinner served in lodge dining room. Beer and wine served. No children under 12 years. No pets. Ranch activities include riding, fishing, hiking, tennis, natural hot-springs swimming pool, and outdoor barbecue once a week. Sawtooth Wilderness pack trips can be arranged.

DIRECTIONS: From Sun Valley 50 miles north on Rte. 75. From Boise Rte. 21 into Stanley. Take right onto Rte. 75, drive 10 miles south of Stanley. Watch for sign.

Salmon
GREYHOUSE INN
IDAHO

Idaho's countryside reveals a fantasy country inn

The inn is about six hundred feet from the Salmon River, "the river of no return." It will be hard to return to any place after staying at The Greyhouse. It is a fantasy come true: a Victorian style farmhouse fronted by sunflowers and lavepera, propped against the aspen and serviceberry-covered rolling foothills of the Salmon Mountains and the Lemhi range.

The fantasy was not always here. The house was moved from Salmon, twelve miles away. Vera and Robert Slicton came upon it after searching Montana, Nevada, and Wyoming for the house they wanted to restore after retiring.

The upstairs of the 1894 house was restored by the Slictons after having been previously gutted by a series of fires. The Tower suite, a bedroom-sitting

Left: Trout fishing in the Salmon River near the inn.

room, and the other guest room are both furnished with antique furniture and pot-bellied stoves. They share a spacious bathroom the size of a dressing room, complete with claw-footed tub. Homemade rolls and fruit compote are served for breakfast in the sun-filled dining room.

People come here to relax and fish, or ride the rapids on the Salmon River. Riding the rapids requires an adventurous spirit. Staying at the Greyhouse Inn does not.

THE GREYHOUSE INN, Star Rte. Box 16, Salmon, ID 83467; (208) 756-3968; Robert and Vera Slicton, Innkeepers. Western Victorian farm house with 1 room and 1 suite sharing bath. No smoking indoors. Open May through September. Rates: $15 single, $30 double. Continental breakfast included in rates; dinner with wine available on advance notice. Liquor not available but guests may bring their own. No children under 12. No pets. No credit cards accepted. Nearby activities include steelhead and trout fishing, big game hunting, pack trips, jeep trips, and horseback riding.

DIRECTIONS: From Missoula, Montana, take US 93 south. From Sun Valley take Rte. 75 north through Galena Pass to US 93 north. The inn is on US 93 opposite highway marker No. 293.

The Lemhi Mountains are the perfect backdrop to this photogenic Rocky Mountain country inn.

Windfall profits in oil country

When you're "On the Road Again" traveling across I-80 to San Francisco or Salt Lake City, Pine Gables Lodge is a good stopping-off place. In downtown, oil-rich Evanston, an on-again-off-again boom town, Wyoming's only bed and breakfast is built on top of a working oil field. Arthur and Jessie Monroe, the likeable owners, earn about $200 a year in oil royalties and pay $1.37 a month windfall profits tax.

Most of the present lodging in the area was financed by oil companies for an influx of workers and passers-through, but Pine Gables Lodge was built by a banker a century ago. The gabled Victorian wood frame house has an extensive collection of Eastlake period pieces. Popular from 1870 to 1890, this post-Victorian furniture style was designed in England by Charles Locke Eastlake. It is distinguished by rectilinear simplicity, incising, spindling, and relief carving. Dressers, bedsteads, chests, and two fireplaces are Eastlake examples worth noting here.

Another windfall are some of the nearby places frequented by locals and recommended by the Monroes, like the Back Forty, a popular restaurant. Handsomely structured from outsized logs, with antelope and deer heads on its walls, it features great tasting ribs and roast beef. Later try Billy's, a rambling country and western place, where you can shoot pool with cowboys, toe-tap to great music, glimpse briefly-clad barmaids, and dance your heart out. Among others, Dolly Parton, Barbara Mandrell, and Willie Nelson have appeared there.

PINE GABLES LODGE, 1049 Center St., Evanston, WY 82930; (307) 789-2069; Arthur and Jessie Monroe, Innkeepers. A gabled Victorian home, built in 1883, fronted by a sun porch. Open year round. Six rooms with private and shared baths. Rates: $28.50 single, $34.50 double, including Continental breakfast. No bar, guests are welcome to bring own liquor. Children under 12 free. Pets welcome. Visa, MasterCard, Diners Club accepted. Golf, hiking, and skiing available nearby, along with Fossil Butte National Monument, and Fort Bridger State Museum.

DIRECTIONS: From Salt Lake City 84 miles on I-80 east to first Evanston exit; follow Lincoln Way for 6 blocks to 11th St. Inn is on right hand side.

Once the meeting place of the Womens' Christian Temperance Movement.

A gourmet center in big game country

Mike Self bought this old stagecoach stop after the recession k.o.'d his golf business in California. Joined by Doug and Kathy Campbell, friends from Wyoming University, the partners launched a major renovation. Plaster was stripped to expose old brickwork, rooms were remodeled, and brass and oak furniture was added. Stained glass was hung throughout. Suddenly the Wolf had seventeen pleasing guest rooms, two charming dining rooms, and a cocktail lounge in its original old bar.

Bought to be turned into a "nice restaurant," the Wolf lives up to its owners' aspirations. The inch-thick tender rib steaks, juicy prime ribs, deep fried wall-eye pike, and cheese cake are reputed to be the best in the county. On Thursday everyone in town comes to lunch for Kathy's Mexican plate special: chicken enchiladas, chili releno, tostados, and the burritos she learned to make in California.

Hunting and fishing are the biggest drawing card in this area, a true sportsman's paradise. Trophy elk, deer, and antelope hunts, or fishing and float trips are arranged by the outfitting and guide service run by the Wolf's partners along with friend Ed Beattie, a disaffected forest ranger. Hunters have the option of staying at the Wolf or at hunting camps set up in Snowy Range high country, the Sierra Madres, or Medicine Bow National Forest.

Mike Self's parents run a hotel and restaurant on the other side of the mountains. Hotel Wolf is giving them competition.

HOTEL WOLF, Saratoga, WY 82331; (307) 326-5525; Mike Self and Doug Campbell, Innkeepers. Western 3 story brick hotel with dormers. Open all year except Thanksgiving and Christmas days. Seventeen rooms with private and shared baths. Rates: $12 to $16 single, $16 to $22 double. Only lunch and dinner served. Bar. Children under 12 free. No pets. Visa and MasterCard accepted. Good hunting and fishing in area, outfitting arranged through hotel. Natural hot springs. Open year round. Cross-country skiing in winter.

DIRECTIONS: Saratoga is on Rte. 130, 20 miles south of I-80 or 80 miles west of Laramie on Rte. 130.

Built in 1893 by Frederick Wolf as a stagecoach stop.

VIRGINIAN HOTEL

Medicine Bow   **WYOMING**

"When you call me that, *smile!*"

Named after Owen Wister's novel *The Virginian*, the hotel was built in 1909, on the site of the saloon where the villain Trampas confronts the Virginian over a card game. Trampas makes the mistake of calling the Virginian a "son of a bitch." The Virginian draws his pistol aimlessly over the table and utters the immortal line, "When you call me that, *smile!*" As you might expect, there is a Wister dining room and suite in the hotel and a couple of his autographed photos.

Running the hotel for the last four years is rancher Dick Mowery, whose cattle provide the restaurant with choice steaks. Good hearty food, cooked home-style and plentiful, is served up three meals a day. Mowery has spent time and money remodeling the place, bringing it back to the turn-of-the-century look that gambler Gus Grimm created when he built it. A 1940s modernization is being replaced by hardwood

The original "Home on the Range" country.

floors, wainscotting, restored tin ceilings, and period wallpapers. The old Victorian furniture remains as it was when the sporting crowd occupied these rooms.

The Virginian, tallest building in Medicine Bow, looms over the flat, empty plains in a haunting and beautiful vastness of space. Train whistles echo through town and the wind is constantly blowing—so much so that the government has funded a project in alternative energy, and wind turbines stand over Medicine Bow's prairies like giant sentinels.

This is the West: a land of real cowboys and Indians, grass and sagebrush covered prairies, red-and-purple-striped badlands, free-roaming buffalo, elk, deer, and antelope, and huge cattle ranches. The Virginian offers a chance to see what the Old West was like and confront the new. "Occasionally cowhands ride their horses into the bar and we have to clean up after them," Mowery tells us. You know you're in the West.

Left: The Owen Wister suite.

VIRGINIAN HOTEL, P.O. Box 176, Medicine Bow, WY 82329; (307) 379-2377; Dick Mowery, Owner. A 1907 stone building in a town of 850 people. Open year round. There are 32 rooms and 4 suites with private and shared baths; 17 modern cabins with baths. Rates: $18 to $26 per person. Dining room serves three meals. Saloon. Children welcome. Pets only in cabins. Visa and MasterCard accepted. Year-round indoor swimming pool in town, big game hunting in season, dinosaur graveyard nearby. Medicine Bow National Forest.

DIRECTIONS: On US 30 off I-80 in southeast Wyoming.

MINER'S DELIGHT INN

Lander   **WYOMING**

Fine food by reservation only

Many years ago, before innkeepers Paul Newman and his wife Georgina came to Wyoming, they lived in New York. Shoe box after shoe box of cookies arrived at their doorstep, for actor Paul Newman, from a lady in Iowa. Now the Newmans are well known in their own right, with nationally known gourmet magazines acclaiming their restaurant at Miner's Delight.

Food is the keynote here but Georgina thinks "gourmet food" is an over-used term. "Fine food" is what they offer, anything from prime ribs to boned chicken Milano with jumbo shrimp. The latter is prepared by the Newmans working together, with Paul boning the chicken breasts and sautéeing them, and Georgina preparing the shrimp and the wine sauce. An entrée is selected for the day and five-course dinners are served by reservation only.

The Newmans perfected their cooking skills after leaving careers in writing and advertising and moving out here in the early sixties. They bought the old "Carpenter Hotel" and spent four years restoring it after Miss Ellen, its proprietor, died. Originally intended for their private residence, they decided to make more dollars and sense of it, and spent time in Park City, Vail, and Aspen, learning to cook.

The rustic log exterior of the hotel belies its interior furnishings—white muslin covered couches, flokati

Left: The inviting dining room, *above,* and a comfortable corner of the bar, *below.*

and Navajo rugs, gold and white floral table cloths, high-back wicker and iron bedsteads, and genuine old crazy quilt and fan-patterned quilts. In short the sitting room, two dining rooms, and bars are elegant in a casual way. Three guest rooms are available in the inn, as well as accommodations in four cabins that have no plumbing. (Basins of hot water are brought in for washing up).

The Newmans, both serious fishermen, claim the fly fishing in the Sweetwater River is the best in the West. Located in Lander, "Where the rails end and the trails begin," this place is worth seeking out.

MINER'S DELIGHT INN, Box 205, Atlantic City Rte., Lander, WY 82520; (307) 332-3513; Paul and Georgina Newman, Innkeepers. A restored pioneer hotel open May 1st through New Year's Eve, Thursday through Sunday only. Three bedrooms with baths and twin beds. Four homesteader cabins with 2 double beds each, no indoor plumbing. Dinner only meal served, by reservation only. Continental breakfast for guests. Rates on request. Teenagers only. No pets. No credit cards accepted. Vicinity offers fly fishing on Sweetwater River, the Shoeshone National Forest and winter sports area, and the Oregon Trail.

DIRECTIONS: From Lander 29 miles south on Rte. 28 to graveled road marked Atlantic City; 3 miles to town and inn.

IRMA HOTEL

Cody   **WYOMING**

A poster in the Buffalo Bill Historical Center.

Buffalo Bill's legacy is alive and well

At the Irma Hotel you are close to the man who embodied the spirit of the Old West—Buffalo Bill Cody. The extravagant hotel was named after his surviving daughter Irma, and built in Cody, a town he promoted at the doorstop of Yellowstone National Park.

Before that, Cody had done everything a man could do in the West, and more. He rode for the Pony Express at fourteen, prospected, was a frontiersman, fought in the Civil War, was an Indian scout, and worked as a guide. He earned his nickname working for the Kansas Pacific Railroad, shooting twelve buffalo a day to feed the crew.

Cody realized the end of the Old West was only a matter of time, and he figured that when it was gone, folks would be wondering what it had been like. A showman by nature, he envisioned perpetuating his own romantic vision of it. In 1883, Buffalo Bill's Wild West Show was born, a forerunner of modern-day rodeos. Cowboys on bucking broncos, Annie

Oakley shooting a hundred flying targets without a miss, and Indians (including Sitting Bull)—all rein-acted the dramatic episodes that made the West legendary. The show played to great crowds here and abroad, at places like the Chicago World's Fair, the Vatican, and Queen Victoria's Golden Jubilee.

Fifteen original suites from the 1902 Irma remain, each named after a Wyoming hero, and all restored with period wallpapers and furnished with original old bedsteads, dressers, tables, rockers, and marble sinks. The suite that Buffalo Bill designed for himself, and to which he returned between wild west shows, is available, along with an opportunity to sleep in the showman's bed.

In the Buffalo Bill Historical Center in Cody, you can find memorabilia given to him by Grand Duke Alexis of Russia, General Philip Sheridan, Wild Bill Hickock, and Edward, Prince of Wales, who once rode shotgun on a stagecoach driven by Buffalo Bill. Seated inside the stagecoach were the kings of Belgium, Saxony, Denmark, and Greece.

Crowds went wild over Buffalo Bill and his legacy lives on in our love of the Old West as he knew it.

A detail of the famous Cherrywood bar.

Left: The Irma was opened in 1902, cost $80,000, and had a telephone in every room.

IRMA HOTEL, 1192 Sheridan Ave., Cody, WY 82414; (307) 587-4221; Douglas R. Greenway, Manager. A historic western hotel built out of cut sandstone in the early 1900s. Open year round except Christmas day and New Year's day. Forty-one rooms, including 15 period rooms, with private bath, TV, and telephone. Rates: single $30 to $41, double $33 to $45. Restaurant serves 3 meals daily. Children under 8 free. Pets not encouraged. MasterCard, Visa, American Express accepted. Nearby there is a golf course, the Buffalo Bill Historical Center, and rodeos in summer. Fifty miles east of Yellowstone National Park.

DIRECTIONS: Cody is in northwest Wyoming on US 16. The hotel is on the main street.

OLD FAITHFUL INN

Rustic lodgings in geyser country

Watching Old Faithful.

There is no doubt that this is a country inn in the best western tradition. A huge building, built of logs, with a massive stone fireplace in a rustic lobby which soars to the building's full height, the Old Faithful Inn is breathtaking to see. The only trouble is that you have to share it with 90,000 other guests a year, all visitors to Yellowstone, one of the most popular national parks in the country. Traffic in the park is bumper-to-bumper and tediously slow during the summer months. Spring and fall would be a better time to go, when it is much easier to enjoy the animals, vegetation, and infinite variety of natural sights.

Situated directly overlooking Old Faithful, you can watch from the inn as the geyser erupts approximately every hour. In fact, the inn is so perfectly situated that it has had to expand twice since it was opened in 1904. The original building contains the guest rooms most sought after, because of their views and their more rustic interiors, although they mostly have shared baths.

The park itself is approximately 80 miles wide by 100 miles long, much larger than a lot of visitors imagine. The inn stresses that you should plan to stay more than one night if you really want to see Yellowstone. There is Geyser Country, Roosevelt Country, Lake Country, and Canyon Country, all of

Left: Designed by a young architect, Robert C. Reamer, the inn's lobby soars to a height of 85 feet and is lit by dormer windows.

which constitute one of the world's great natural extravaganzas. Small wonder the traffic is bumper-to-bumper—it's worth it.

OLD FAITHFUL INN, Yellowstone National Park, WY 82190; (307) 344-7311; TWA Services, Owners. A rustic, western inn, once the largest log building in America, with 140 rooms, mostly with shared baths. Two newer wings contain an additional 210 rooms, about 70 with private baths. Summer season rates (mid-May to mid-October): $49 deluxe with bath, $38 with bath, $24 with shared bath; same rate double or single, $5 extra person. Children welcome (under 11 free). Pets welcome but must be supervised at all times. Dining room with fixed hours serves 3 meals. Bear Pit bar serves liquor. Visa, MasterCard, Diners Club, American Express accepted. On your doorstep are the wonders of Yellowstone.

DIRECTIONS: Follow roads 50 miles from east and south entrances to park, or 30 miles from west entrance, or 55 miles from north entrance, to Old Faithful geyser.

NEVADA CITY HOTEL
FAIRWEATHER INN

Nevada City
Virginia City

MONTANA

Two restored towns, totally authentic

The Old West lives on here in these two gold-mining towns, where history began in 1863 when prospectors discovered gold. Virginia City is preserved as it was, an outstanding collection of boom-town architecture. Nevada City, a ghost town, is augmented with buildings from all parts of Montana, all painstakingly restored. When scenes from *Little Big Man* were filmed here, the town was so complete in its authenticity that only one false front was added. Both towns, one-and-a-half miles apart, have been meticulously stocked with authentic fittings, fixtures, period furnishings, and merchandise. Together they are a walk-through museum—the Old West suspended in time.

The restoration of both towns is the work of one man, nurtured by his love of Montana's past and his vision of what could be done to preserve it. Charles A. Bovey, along with his wife, Sue Ford Bovey, collected everything from shoe hooks to the buildings where shoe hooks were sold, and forged their dream.

The FAIRWEATHER INN in Virginia City is an old western two-story white clapboard building with a balcony overlooking the center of town. It is named after William Fairweather, the first prospector to discover gold here. Decorated in western style, it

A Fairweather Inn interior.

provides guests with a genuine feeling of the period. Most rooms do not have a private bath, just the traditional washstand.

The NEVADA CITY HOTEL, constructed of chinked logs, was built in Bollinger, Montana, back in 1862. Once used as a post office, it was moved piece by piece to Nevada City in 1958. Furnished with old Victorian pieces, it recaptures the flavor of the period, as do two large guest rooms. There are twelve rooms with more modern accommodations, and fourteen replica miners' log cabins, with sod roofs, which offer additional accommodations with modern facilities.

Linking both towns is the Alder Gulch work train, a narrow gauge line carrying passengers to and fro. At the end of the line, in Nevada City, the Steam Railroad Museum has a fine collection of rolling stock from the days when railroads were the lifeblood of the country.

Being here is eerie. No one is around pointing things out. There is just you and the Old West, and you feel you are part of it.

One of two guest rooms in the Nevada City Hotel completely furnished in period decor.

Left: The Nevada City Hotel. OVERLEAF: A few of the many buildings in Nevada City preserved and restored inside and out.

NEVADA CITY HOTEL, Nevada City, MT 59755; (406) 843-5382; Nancy Mitman, Manager. Open June 15 to Sept. 6. Fourteen rooms with baths; 14 cabins with showers. Rates: $24 single, $27 double. Star Bakery on premises open for all meals. No liquor served but guests may bring own. Children under 12 free. Ask about pets. No credit cards.
FAIRWEATHER INN, Box 338, Virginia City, MT 59755; (406) 843-5377; Nancy Mitman, Manager. Open June 15 to Sept. 6. Fourteen rooms with private and shared baths. Rates: $15 to $24 single, $17 to $27 double. No bar or restaurant. Guests welcome to bring own liquor. Children under 12 free. No credit cards accepted.
DIRECTIONS: Both towns are mid-way between Butte and Bozeman on Montana Rte. 287.

LONE MOUNTAIN RANCH

Big Sky   MONTANA

Where the wilderness matters

Western furnishings and Indian artifacts have transformed the old cattle ranch into one of Montana's best guest ranches.

This is more than a ranch. Although it offers heated log cabins with fireplaces, family-style gourmet food in a western-style dining hall (including table-carved rib roast, sauce bernaise, and bananas flambé), cookouts, hayrides, horsepack trips into the Yellowstone wilderness, Nordic skiing on thirty-five miles of groomed trails, and fishing in the Gallatin River, it is also a monument to its owners' love of the wilderness. And you leave here with a concern for the land.

Everything is conducted in that spirit by wranglers, naturalists, and guides. Concerned with the effect of horses on the high-country environment, the Schaaps limit the number of their pack animals to avoid overgrazing its delicate vegetation. Fisherman are encouraged to keep only the fish they can eat and photography, a major interest here, includes learning non-threatening postures to minimize disturbing big game animals.

Schapp's favorite thing is conducting ride-hikes up into country so steep a horse can't negotiate it. "You tie the horses up and climb higher than you could get any other way." Mountain sheep, goats, sub-Alpine firs, and white-bark pine reveal themselves amid gardens of Alpine wildflowers: moss campion, cinquefoil, mountain heather. Plants, growing one to two feet in the lower elevations, grow only one inch on these eleven thousand foot peaks. "You feel good climbing to the top of a peak and learning about life as you have never seen it."

Then there are the extras, the things that firmly establish this place as a wilderness learning center. Big game photographer Tom McBride conducts a special workshop for one week in June, complete with shooting sessions, darkroom techniques, and technical skill instruction. Extension courses on the Yellowstone ecosystem originate here, sponsored by science museums and universities. Overnight field trips to Yellowstone explore its wildlife, geology, and lore, and are combined with skiing at Old Faithful, gourmet bonfire trail lunches, and photo session clinics—all supervised by geology professors, naturalists, and members of the ranch's Nordic staff. Information for seasonal offerings should be requested well in advance, as should reservations for staying here.

Growing up in Wyoming's high country, Bob Schaap had his first love affair there—with the mountains—an ongoing romance that his wife Viv shares with him. Briefly transplanted to the East and high-tech computer technology, the Schaaps have returned to the mountains where things feel right and matter to them.

LONE MOUNTAIN RANCH, Box 145, Big Sky, MT 59716; (406) 995-4644; Bob and Vivian Schaap, Owners. Ranch-style lodgings with a rustic flavor. Closed October through 2nd week in December and mid-April through May. Twelve cabins, all with baths. A variety of weekly and fortnightly packages are available, including gourmet meals. Seasonal rates, with many options, starting at $495 single, $407 for second person. Shorter stays are possible. Visa, MasterCard, American Express accepted. Children and pets welcome. Recreation on grounds includes horseback riding and Nordic skiing. Nearby, golf, fishing, and tennis are available.

DIRECTIONS: Frontier Airlines and Northwest Orient fly to Bozeman. Pickup included in rates. Driving, south from Bozeman 35 miles on US 191. Turn right on road to Big Sky Resort and turn right to ranch after 4 miles.

Left: Above, wranglers herding horses to pasture from the corral. *Below,* the cookouts are as popular as the moonlight safaris and the mule-drawn wagon rides.

A secret treasure finally revealed

Larry Edwards, the amazing chef who has put Chico on the map.

The big draw here is the food. Since buying into the place six years ago, chef Larry Edwards, an MIT graduate, has brought artichokes and gazpacho to steak-and-potatoes country. Folks from Billings flock here from 135 miles away to have beef Wellington and Zinfandel—then drive home. People in need of a gourmet fix fly planes in from Salt Lake City and Denver—they land on the highway, tie down near the barn, then relish the sole en croute and savor the Pouilly Fuissé.

Mike and Eve Art are responsible for the Chico's rising star. After leaving his chain of 36 men's clothing stores in Cleveland, they bought the Chico and started revitalizing it. The large hot-springs pool was cleaned up, the saloon refurbished, private baths added to rooms, barn siding installed in the dining room, and two chalets built to accommodate guests. After eight years of neglect the Chico started looking good, without losing its old western charm.

Before the hotel went up at the turn of the century, prospectors used the hot springs for bathing and washing their duds. The old Chico boasted of a circular hot-springs plunge, an open-air dance pavilion, and a free-standing saloon. Touted as a health resort and natatorium—"the best in the country"—it was recommended for sufferers of stomach trouble, blood disease, and rheumatism.

Thirty miles north of Yellowstone Park, the Chico is surrounded on three sides by the Absoroka range of the Rocky Mountains. Riding the scenic trails and pack trips into Yellowstone Park are arranged by outfitters at the lodge. Single overnights or weekly excursions are available and there are fly fishing float trips down the Yellowstone River.

Recently, in response to a magazine article on the Chico Hot Springs, a reader wrote: "I am very distressed with your article on Chico Hot Springs here in Montana. I have been trying for two years to keep that place a secret." That's how good it is.

The hot-springs pool.

Left: Chico is like a magnet that draws people from everywhere. Its bar and restaurant, seen below, are legendary.

CHICO HOT SPRINGS LODGE, Pray, MT 59065; (406) 333-4411; Mike and Eve Art, Larry Edwards, Innkeepers. A 60 room lodge with an interesting mixture of early western hotel, modern motel, chalet, and log cabin accommodations. Open year round. Variety of rooms available in main lodge and motel. Rates: $18 to $25 single, $24 to $36 double. Private and shared baths. Chalets and cabin sleeping 6 to 10 people, $90 to $110 per night. Gourmet restaurant serves breakfast and dinner; snack bar. Bar. Children welcome (no charge under 6). Pets not encouraged. Visa and MasterCard accepted. Live entertainment on weekends. Activities include swimming, riding, fly fishing, rafting, hiking, and hot-springs pool. Outfitting arranged through hotel. Thirty miles from north entrance to Yellowstone.

DIRECTIONS: From Bozeman take I-90 east, exit 333 at Livingstone to US 89 south. Exit left at Emigrant to Chico Hot Springs.

LAZY K BAR RANCH

Big Timber   **MONTANA**

A working ranch for classy dudes

Four generations of Van Cleves have run this ranch, starting with Paul Van Cleve, who came here in 1880 as a civil engineer to lay out the route for the Northern Pacific Railway. When he reached the present site of Big Timber he "kinda liked it" and decided to stay.

Dude ranching started at the Lazy K in 1922 after eastern friends of Princeton-educated Van Cleves descended on the place, making it the third or fourth dude ranch in the country. Grandfather Van Cleve went on to help start the Dude Ranchers' Association and served two terms as president, as did his son Spike and Spike's son Tack, the present owner.

Tack (Paul IV) and his mother, Barbara, manage the 20,000 acre Lazy K Bar Ranch. Coming here from Melville, you follow a single-lane dirt road which goes on for miles through a sea of rolling grassland, stretching as far as your eye can see, to the snow-capped Crazy Mountains in the distance. Finally the complex appears: beautiful hand-hewn log cabins built up and down the mountainside and covered in white-flowered vines. Each of the cabins is different, but most have a porch and sitting room, and all have magnificent views of Big Timber Mountain and the river below.

Matching sets of carved heavy oak furniture from a Scottish castle command the lodge's high-beamed living room, and the billiard table was found by a hired hand in a sporting house.

Meals are home-style cooking from old family recipes, and are served up generously, family style. Delicious steaks from grass-fed cows as well as pork, dairy products, and vegetables originate here. There are heaping casseroles and bowls of garden fresh salad, and a homemade molasses and cornmeal Annadamer bread is mouth watering and addictive.

This is a riding ranch, and all of the quarter horses are bred here. Riding over range land, foothills, or high plains, hundred-mile views span the horizon. There is trout fishing in the Sweet Grass Creek, swimming in the heated pool, and a Saturday night square dance. Impromptu talent shows uncover hoofers, magicians, and jugglers.

Left: Guest cabins, *above,* are built up and down the mountain side. The main lounge, *below,* is a classic of its kind.

The corral of a working ranch that raises its own quarter horses.

Most entertaining of all is Tack Van Cleve, the Will Rogers of the Lazy K Bar. Just like his father, Spike, he is an excellent spinner of yarns, telling stories that have been lovingly gathered and passed on from one generation to the next. The story of this ranch and its family unfolds in the grand tradition.

LAZY K BAR RANCH, Box 550, Big Timber, MT 59011; (406) 537-4404; the Van Cleve Family, Innkeepers. Make reservations 5 months in advance; references required. Open last week of June though Labor Day. Twenty-three log cabins, 1 to 4 bedrooms; most with living room and private bath. Rates: $375 to $425 a week single occupancy, including meals and exclusive use of a saddle horse. Other rates on request. Family-style dining room serves 3 hearty meals. No bar, but guests may bring own liquor. Children welcome. No pets. No credit cards accepted. Activities include riding, stockwork, fishing, swimming, hiking, and Sat. night square dances..

DIRECTIONS: From Billings I-90 west and Boseman I-90 east to Big Timber. Turn north onto US 191 for 11 miles. At large sign "Big Timber Canyon" make left onto gravel road and continue to small "Big Timber Canyon" sign. Turn right and continue on gravel road to ranch. Ranch provides transportation to and from Billings and Bozeman airports for $90 a trip (100 miles).

IZAAK WALTON INN

Essex   **MONTANA**

PHOTOGRAPHED BY PHILIP LIEF

A railroad buff's delight

For those who love to watch the trains go by, the Izaak Walton Inn offers the opportunity to do just that in surroundings harkening back to the days of steam locomotives. Fifteen trains, including Amtrak, pass daily on the tracks next to the inn, and other nearby sights include trestles, tunnels, and avalanche sheds. The inn itself was built in 1939 by the Great Northern Railway as a lodging house for employees. Since 1974 the Izaak Walton has been run by Sid and Millie Goodrich, Michigan natives, for whom a friendly cup of coffee with a local real estate agent marked the beginning of a new career.

The Goodriches' enthusiasm for both innkeeping and railroading is apparent in the lobby and lounge

Left: The Goodriches, innkeepers since 1974.

area, which contains Sid's collection of railroad memorabilia and Millie's collection of clocks. Geared to the keen appetites of railroad employees, meals are well-prepared and satisfying with whole-wheat breads, homemade soups and desserts, and Chinese specialties to vary the selection of beef and chicken. Guest rooms are paneled with knotty pine and simply but adequately furnished with rooms on the track side in the most demand. And for those seeking diversion in between trains, there is hiking in the Great Bear Wilderness area, and in the winter, cross-country skiing.

IZAAK WALTON INN, Box 675, Essex, MT 59916; tell your operator to call Essex number 1, via Great Falls, Montana. Sid and Millie Goodrich, Innkeepers. Blend of English Tudor and western railroad style. Open year round. Twenty-four standard and deluxe rooms. Private and shared baths. Rates: $17 and $24 single, $22 and $34 double. Restaurant and bar. Children welcome. No pets. Visa and MasterCard accepted. Sauna, hiking, Nordic skiing, and fishing. Railfans spend much time photographing trains.

DIRECTIONS: 60 miles east of Kallispell on US 2 or ½ mile off Rte. 2 between East and West Glacier at southern end of Glacier Park. Sign is for Essex only, not the inn.

The perfect inn for photographing trains going by.

MANY GLACIER HOTEL	LAKE McDONALD LODGE	
Glacier Park	GLACIER PARK LODGE	MONTANA

ALL GLACIER PARK PHOTOGRAPHS BY PHILIP LIEF

Amid the grandeur of glaciers

With jagged, snow-capped peaks, sparkling lakes, dense forests, and lush Alpine meadows, Glacier National Park offers some of the most breathtaking scenery in the country. It also has three fine old hotels built by the Great Northern Railway in the early 1900s. Then, such a visit usually began with a stop at the GLACIER PARK LODGE, located in East Glacier just outside the park boundary. The showpiece of the three, this hotel was and still is noted for its lovely Alpine flower gardens and for the immense supporting timbers visible in the lobby and on the verandas.

Within the park itself, MANY GLACIER HOTEL occupies a choice spot overlooking Swiftcurrent Lake and has easy access to most trails. "Many" is also the largest of the three hotels. The hotel has a Swiss chalet motif, but the music is straight from Broadway. Each year the staff, recruited from music and drama

Left: The monumental lobby of Glacier Park Lodge, ringed with forty-foot supporting timbers.

departments all over the country, mounts a major Broadway musical, and there's live music in the lounges, and singing waiters and waitresses in the dining hall.

Smaller and more intimate in atmosphere, LAKE MCDONALD LODGE is located at the western end of the park on the shores of its largest lake. Inside, stuffed moose heads and other wildlife decorate the lobby and dining hall, recalling the hotel's origins as a hunting lodge. Under the auspices of Greyhound Food Management, Inc., rooms in all the hotels are being renovated, but visitors cannot expect the first-rate cuisine characteristic of the Great Northern in its heyday.

GLACIER PARK LODGE, East Glacier, MT 59434; (406) 226-5551; Ron Duncan, Innkeeper, 155 rooms with baths.
LAKE MCDONALD LODGE, Lake McDonald, MT 59921; (406) 888-5431; Richard Earle, Innkeeper. 101 rooms: 32 in lodge, 39 cabins, 30 motel, all with baths.
MANY GLACIER HOTEL, Many Glacier, MT 59936; (406) 732-4411; Ian B. Tippet, Innkeeper. 232 rooms, most with baths.

All are open June 10 to Sept. 15, have restaurants and bars, accept children and pets and Visa and MasterCard. For reservations, rates, and directions call: *summer* (800) 332-9351; *winter* (602) 795-0377.

Many Glacier Lodge, looking out on Swiftcurrent Lake.

GRANITE PARK CHALET
SPERRY CHALET

Glacier Park

MONTANA

Two unique chalets in remote high country

A dramatic, ever-changing cloud- and mountainscape, a silence broken only by the shrill whistle of a marmot, an exhilarating sense of being "above it all" at 7,000 feet—these are among the rewards awaiting visitors to Glacier's high country, who will also find unique accommodations in the form of two stone chalets built around 1914 by the Great Northern Railway.

Both can only be reached by trail, "packing in and packing out," and both offer rustic but adequate accommodations in a spectacular setting. Furnished with iron beds and turn-of-the-century wooden furniture, rooms are lit by kerosene lamps at Sperry and by candlelight at Granite. Hearty meals, served family-style in the dining room, are the occasion for much convivial sharing of experiences.

Right: Rocky Mountain goats and bighorn sheep seen on the trail to Sperry Chalet. OVERLEAF: From Granite Park Chalet, there's a long long trail awinding into the land of your dreams.

Vistors to SPERRY usually make the side trip to the glacier, hiking to the headwall, up a steep stone stairway, and then across the snowfields to the glacier itself. Those who come to GRANITE PARK usually do so for the experience of hiking the "High-line" trail, carved out of the sheer face of the Garden Wall, with magnificent views, but dizzying drops.

Both chalets have been managed by the same family, the Ludings, for nearly thirty years. A cheerful, no-nonsense person, Kay Luding was once asked how she knew the number of pies to bake for dinner. "I just look down the trail and see who's coming," she replied.

SPERRY AND GRANITE PARK CHALETS, Belton Park Chalets, Inc., Box 188, West Glacier, MT 59936; (406) 888-5511; Kay and Lanny Luding, Innkeepers. Stone chalets in remote parts of Glacier Park. Open July 1 to Labor Day. Write for reservations before April 1. There are 18 rooms at Sperry, 11 rooms at Granite. Rates: $32.50 per person, $27 per child, including all meals. No liquor served but guests may bring their own. No pets. No credit cards accepted.

DIRECTIONS: Chalets must be reached by hiking or saddle horses. Ask for information when making reservations.

A spectacular view of Granite Park Chalet, 6700 feet up.